# The Storified Jokes of Nasreddin Hodja

*Wit and Wisdom Unveiled*

## Memet T Zunun

Uyghur Language Studies

London 2007

1

# Preface

In this book, I warmly invite you on a journey through the timeless tales of Nasreddin Hodja, a beloved figure of humour and profound wisdom. Through my storytelling, I aim to present these age-old jokes fresh and captivatingly, offering a new perspective on the stories and delving into their profound wisdom. You are encouraged to explore these stories with an open mind and a curious heart.

Nasreddin Hodja's tales, like a thread that weaves through the fabric of humanity, have traversed generations, transcended cultural boundaries, and captivated the hearts and minds of people from all walks of life. Their significance extends universally from being confined to a specific time or place. Each story holds a hidden treasure, a nugget of wisdom waiting to be discovered and contemplated, connecting us to a shared cultural heritage.

In this book, I have storified Nasreddin Hodja's jokes, weaving them into a tapestry of narratives that entertain and provoke thought and reflection. Through my point of view, I shed light on the stories' more profound meanings, offering insights that can significantly enhance our understanding and appreciation of Nasreddin Hodja's tales, enriching our knowledge and broadening our perspectives.

By presenting these stories in a new light, I hope to ignite a spark of curiosity within you, encouraging you to engage with the tales on a deeper level. As you embark on this journey, allow yourself to explore the lessons and wisdom they offer, for it is within these ancient anecdotes that timeless truths lie hidden.

Beyond their entertainment value, Nasreddin Hodja's stories possess the power to inspire critical thinking, challenge social norms, and foster cultural understanding and tolerance. They teach us to find humour in the face of adversity and to embrace simplicity in wisdom.

Through the medium of this book, I aspire to significantly contribute to the study and appreciation of Nasreddin Hodja's tales. My sincerest hope is that by delving into these storified jokes and the accompanying insights, readers will not only discover a renewed appreciation for the enduring legacy of Nasreddin Hodja but also be intellectually stimulated and engaged in exploring the wisdom he imparts.

So, embark on this journey with an open mind and a willingness to delve into the stories that have captivated countless hearts throughout the ages. Let us explore the depths of Nasreddin Hodja's wit and wisdom together, for within these pages lie lessons that not only transcend time but also have the power to transform our lives, inspiring us and filling us with hope.

# Contents

# Nasreddin Hodja

Good day, everyone!

Today, we dive into a fascinating piece of cultural heritage that bridges time and geography: the figure of "Hodja," a title with deep roots in Middle Eastern and Central Asian cultures. Specifically, we will explore Nasreddin Hodja, a legendary character whose wit and wisdom have transcended borders and generations.

The term "Hodja" originates from the Arabic word "Khawaja," meaning "master" or "teacher," and is used as a mark of respect for scholars and religious leaders. One of the most celebrated figures with this title is Nasreddin Hodja. Known by various names like Nasrettin, Nesirdin, and Mullah Nasreddin, this iconic character is a staple of Turkish, Middle Eastern, and Central Asian folklore.

Though the precise details of Nasreddin Hodja's life remain mysterious, he is believed to have lived between the 12th and 15th centuries. His birthplace is commonly considered Hortu in Turkey, but his stories have travelled far beyond, resonating in regions as diverse as the Balkans and China.

Nasreddin Hodja is celebrated for his sharp wit and cleverness. He often uses humour to convey moral and philosophical lessons. His anecdotes, filled with satire and insight, are set in a specific cultural and historical context, which is crucial to understanding their significance. For instance, his story of riding a donkey backwards critiques the societal norms of his time. He highlights human nature's quirks and flaws through his stories, making complex ideas accessible and entertaining.

In the Uyghur community, he is known as "Nasreddin Ependi," in Mandarin-speaking China, he is referred to as "Afanti," reflecting his widespread influence. His tales are not just amusing; they offer profound lessons applicable to various aspects of life. His stories are popular not only in Turkey and the Middle East but also in regions as diverse as the Balkans and China, demonstrating the global reach of his influence.

1. **Humour and Perspective:** Hodja's stories teach us the importance of maintaining a sense of humour and perspective, even in tough times.
2. **Critical Thinking:** His clever challenges to social norms encourage us to question authority and think critically.
3. **Simplicity in Wisdom:** His anecdotes often carry deep wisdom wrapped in simplicity, reminding us that significant insights can come from everyday situations.
4. **Moral Lessons:** Many of his tales emphasise virtues like honesty, compassion, and fairness, urging us to reflect on our actions.
5. **Cultural Understanding:** His stories foster empathy and cultural tolerance by highlighting universal human experiences.
6. **Satire and Social Commentary:** Hodja exposes societal flaws and encourages constructive change through satire.
7. **Adaptability:** His resourcefulness in various situations showcases the value of flexibility and resilience.

Nasreddin Hodja's tales resonate today, offering timeless wisdom and entertainment. With their enduring relevance, his stories invite us to approach life with humour, curiosity, and an open mind. As we explore his rich legacy, we uncover valuable lessons that enrich our understanding of human nature and inspire positive change.

Thank you for your interest and for joining me in exploring Nasreddin Hodja's enduring impact. His wisdom and humour remain a guiding light, helping us navigate the complexities of life with a smile and a thoughtful perspective.

# Stories

# Ride the donkey backwards.

Once, Nasreddin Hodja was spotted by a group of people unusually riding his donkey. He was sitting on the donkey facing backwards, with his back towards the front and his face towards the tail. Intrigued by this peculiar sight, the onlookers couldn't help but ask Hodja about his unconventional choice.

"Hodja, why are you riding the donkey backwards?" one of them curiously asked.

With a playful smile, Hodja responded, "Not to see that I'm going in the same direction as the donkey."

Nasreddin Hodja's witty reply held a profound lesson about individuality and the courage to stand out. By riding his donkey backwards, he symbolized his commitment to breaking away from societal norms and thinking independently. His unconventional choice was a metaphor for not following the herd, encouraging others to question the status quo and trust their judgment. This story underscores the value of embracing one's unique perspective, discovering new opportunities, and confidently paving one's path in life. It reminds us to stay true to ourselves and not fear taking a different direction when necessary.

# Whistle

In the small village, a wise man named Nasreddin Hodja lived. He was known for his cleverness and ability to teach essential life lessons through simple stories. One sunny day, Hodja decided to visit the bustling marketplace.

As soon as the children in the village heard about Hodja's plan, they rushed towards him, their faces beaming with excitement. "Hodja, please buy us whistles from the market!" they cried in unison. Hodja chuckled and replied, "My dear children, there's no need to shout so loudly. Give me a moment to gather my thoughts. Alright, I promise to buy the whistles for you."

Among the eager children was a young boy named Ali. He approached Hodja with a determined expression and handed him some money. "Please, Hodja, don't forget to buy me a whistle, too," he said earnestly. Hodja graciously accepted the money and placed it safely in his pocket. With a warm smile, he assured Ali, "Fear not, young one. Your wish will be granted."

Hodja ventured into the lively market, surrounded by vibrant stalls and enthusiastic vendors. He carefully selected the finest whistles, each unique and capable of creating cheerful melodies. The hours passed swiftly as Hodja meticulously completed his purchases, ensuring every child's wish was fulfilled.

As the sun set, the children gathered in the village street, eagerly anticipating Hodja's return. When they finally caught sight of him, their excitement reached new heights. They rushed towards Hodja, their voices merging into a chorus of questions, "Hodja! Where are our whistles? Have you brought them?"

The wise Hodja reached into his pocket and took out a single whistle. He handed it to Ali, the boy entrusted with the money. Looking into Ali's eyes, Hodja spoke gently, "My dear children, here is a whistle for Ali. But before I distribute the rest, I have a small condition. Only those who paid for their whistles may blow them."

A hush fell over the crowd as the children exchanged puzzled glances. Hodja's condition puzzled them, for they had thought their whistles were gifts. Realisation dawned on them, and they understood the wisdom behind Hodja's words.

One by one, the children who had given Hodja their money stepped forward, eagerly ready to claim their whistles. Joyful tunes filled the air as they blew into their shiny new instruments. The other children, who had not contributed their share, watched with longing eyes as their peers revelled in the sweet melodies.

The story's moral is that true joy and satisfaction come from taking responsibility and contributing towards one's desires. Nasreddin Hodja teaches the children the importance of personal investment by making them pay for their whistles. In doing so, he imparts the valuable lesson that rewards and happiness are derived from the generosity of others and one's efforts. The Turkish expression "parayı veren düdüğü çalar" encapsulates this lesson, emphasising that those who contribute hold the authority and control in a given situation. The story encourages a sense of ownership, responsibility, and the understanding that personal investment leads to a deeper appreciation of the rewards gained, reinforcing the value of their efforts and the depth of their relationships.

# Eat, My Coat, Eat

Nasreddin Hodja was invited to a grand banquet in a bustling town. As a humble man, he attended the event in everyday clothes, not wanting to appear flashy or out of place. However, as soon as Hodja arrived at the banquet, he noticed something peculiar. Everyone seemed to disregard his presence, including the host, who failed to acknowledge him.

Feeling ignored and somewhat invisible, Hodja left the banquet and returned home. Realising that perhaps his appearance had played a role in his reception, he hatched a mischievous plan. He wore his most extravagant and fanciest coat, adorned with intricate designs and vibrant colours. Feeling like a peacock, Hodja returned to the banquet, hoping to observe a change in people's behaviour.

To his surprise, Hodja was greeted with warmth and enthusiasm when he entered the banquet hall in his flamboyant coat. The host rushed towards him, extending a warm welcome and inviting him to join the festivities. Hodja was promptly seated at a place of honour, surrounded by people eager to converse and ensure his comfort.

As the banquet progressed, various delectable dishes were served. When it was Hodja's turn to receive his bowl of soup, he dipped the sleeve of his fancy coat into the steaming broth and amusingly exclaimed, "Eat, my coat, eat!"

The host, bewildered by Hodja's peculiar action, approached him curiously and asked for an explanation. The mischievous glint in Hodja's eyes hinted that a valuable lesson would be shared.

"My esteemed host," Hodja began, his voice filled with joy, "allow me to reveal the truth behind my seemingly odd behaviour. When I first arrived at this gathering dressed in my modest attire, no one paid me any attention. I was treated as invisible, and no food or drink offerings came my way."

"However," Hodja continued with a playful smile, "when I returned wearing this magnificent coat, the people who ignored me earlier showered me with warmth and hospitality. It became clear that I was not invited to your banquet but my coat."

The guests, including the host, were taken aback by Hodja's clever observation. They contemplated the truth behind his words and realised the shallowness of their judgment based solely on outward appearances.

With a twinkle in his eye, Hodja concluded, "It is easy to be swayed by material possessions and external appearances. But true worth lies not in the clothes we wear or the trappings we possess. Our character, kindness, and genuine hospitality define us as individuals."

Nasreddin Hodja's story reveals that true worth lies in character, kindness, and genuine hospitality, not material possessions or appearances. By wearing a fancy coat and observing how people treated him differently, Hodja cleverly exposes the shallow nature of such judgments. His humorous act of dipping his sleeve into the soup vividly illustrates the misplaced importance given to superficial aspects. Hodja's message urges us to look beyond external trappings and recognize the true essence of individuals. It highlights the folly of being swayed by material wealth and underscores the significance of character and authentic hospitality. This story reminds us to avoid hasty judgments based on appearances and to value the deeper, more meaningful aspects of human interactions.

# Perfect Wife

When his friend approached him excitedly, Nasreddin Hodja sat in a tea shop. The friend shared the news of his upcoming marriage and inquired if Nasreddin Hodja had ever considered getting married.

Nasreddin Hodja reflected momentarily and responded, "Indeed, I did contemplate marriage. In my youth, the idea appealed to me greatly. I embarked on a journey searching for the perfect wife, hoping to find the ideal companion. I travelled far and wide, exploring different places to pursue this vision."

He continued, "My first stop was Khotan.[1] I encountered a woman of great beauty, kindness, and deep spirituality. However, she lacked worldly knowledge, and I believed a perfect wife should possess inner and outer qualities. So, I continued my quest."

Nasreddin Hodja's eyes sparkled with memories as he recounted his journey, saying, "I then ventured to Turpan.[2], where I met a woman who embodied spirituality and wisdom. She had a deep understanding of the world and its ways. She was beautiful in many aspects, but we struggled to communicate effectively. I realised that genuine connection and communication are vital in a perfect marriage."

He paused momentarily before revealing, "Finally, after much exploration and anticipation, I arrived in Kashgar.[3]. It was there that I found her—the perfect wife. She encompassed spirituality, grace, and beauty in every sense.

---

[1] A city along the Taklamakan Desert
[2] Ancient Oasis City in Uyghur Region
[3] Ancient Oasis City along the Taklamakan Desert in Uyghur Region

She was at ease in both the earthly realm and the realms beyond. I knew deep within my heart that she was the one."

Curious and puzzled, his friend questioned, "Then, Hodja, why did you not marry her? What prevented you from pursuing such a match?"

Nasreddin Hodja sighed and replied with a touch of humour, "Ah, my friend, that is the irony of life. Although I had discovered the perfect wife, she, unfortunately, was searching for the perfect husband."

With a knowing smile, Nasreddin Hodja's tale left his friend pondering a profound truth: the quest for a perfect partner is futile. The story humorously reminds us that true happiness in marriage lies in accepting each other's imperfections and embracing the journey together. Hodja's tale gently underscores the importance of valuing love, understanding, and compatibility over an elusive ideal. It encourages us to seek genuine connections and appreciate the unique qualities in each person. By finding joy in the imperfections of our relationships and cherishing the beauty of shared experiences and acceptance, we discover that a fulfilling marriage comes from embracing the imperfectly perfect journey of love and companionship.

# The Cauldron That Died

Once, Nasreddin Hodja needed a large cooking container. So, he approached his neighbour and kindly asked to borrow the neighbour's copper cauldron. Being a helpful neighbour, the cauldron was lent to Hodja without hesitation, expecting it to be returned in due course.

True to his word, Hodja returned the cauldron on time. However, the neighbour was taken aback when he inspected the cauldron and found a smaller pot. Confused, the neighbour questioned Hodja about the unexpected addition.

With his usual wit and cleverness, Hodja replied calmly, "Ah, my friend, while the cauldron was under my care, it gave birth to a little one. Since you are the rightful owner of the mother cauldron, it only seems fair that you keep its offspring. Besides, it wouldn't be right to separate a child from its mother at such a tender age."

Initially baffled by Hodja's explanation, the neighbour thought that the eccentric Hodja had lost his mind. However, realising that he now possessed a perfectly good little pot at no cost, he decided not to argue further. After all, he had gained something valuable from this peculiar situation.

Sometime later, Hodja again approached his neighbour, requesting to borrow the cauldron. The neighbour, amused by the previous incident, thought, "Why not? Perhaps the cauldron will give birth to another little pot this time."

However, this time, things took an unexpected turn. Days turned into weeks, and no sign of Hodja returning the borrowed cauldron. Growing concerned, the neighbour approached Hodja and demanded the return of his cauldron.

With a sombre expression, Hodja responded, "I'm sorry to say this, my dear friend, but I bring you unfortunate news. Your cauldron has passed away and now rests in her grave."

The neighbour's shock turned into anger, and he shouted, "What nonsense are you speaking? A cauldron cannot live, nor can it die! Return it to me immediately!"

Calmly, Hodja replied, "Hold on for a moment, my friend. This is the same cauldron that not long ago gave birth to a child—a child that you still possess. If a cauldron can bring life into the world, it can also experience its end."

The neighbour's frustration quickly turned to resignation as he realized the logic in Hodja's words. Regrettably, he never saw his cauldron again, as Hodja had artfully turned a borrowing request into a permanent acquisition.

The story's moral is a lesson in accountability and the consequences of our actions. Nasreddin Hodja's clever and humorous tale underscores the importance of being mindful of the responsibilities that come with claiming the benefits of a situation. By turning the borrowed cauldron into a permanent acquisition through clever reasoning, Hodja highlights that if we are quick to enjoy the rewards, we must also be prepared to face the outcomes and obligations that accompany them. The cauldron, once a source of amusement and unexpected gain, becomes a symbolic reminder to choose our words and actions wisely, recognizing their power to shape our experiences and influence how others perceive us. Ultimately, the story serves as a light-hearted yet insightful reminder of the interconnectedness of actions and their consequences in our interactions with others.

# What if it does!

On a peaceful day, Nasreddin Hodja washed a pot of yoghurt near the serene shores of a picturesque lake. As he poured the remnants of the yoghurt into the water, a group of people passing by noticed his peculiar actions. Curiosity piqued, and one couldn't resist the opportunity to mock Hodja.

"Hodja, what on earth are you doing?" the man inquired, unable to contain his amusement.

With a twinkle in his eye, Hodja calmly replied, "I am turning the lake into yogurt."

Laughter erupted among the onlookers, their amusement growing at Hodja's seemingly absurd statement. The man who had questioned him sneered, "Can a mere dollop of yogurt ferment such a vast lake? Surely, you jest!"

Undeterred by their scepticism, Hodja responded with a mischievous grin, "You never know, my friend. Perhaps it might happen. But think for a moment, what if it does!"

Hodja's cryptic response hung in the air, causing the laughter to subside and the mocking smiles to fade. Beneath his playful banter lay a profound meaning. From that day forward, those who witnessed Hodja's act became more open-minded, embracing that greatness can emerge from the most unexpected places. The Turkish expression "ya tutarsa," meaning "What if it does," reflects this lesson, encouraging optimism about potential future events. Nasreddin Hodja's simple yet thought-provoking response forever changed their perspective, urging them to approach life's uncertainties with an open mind and a readiness to explore endless possibilities.

# A Shared Vision

In the bustling bazaar, Nasreddin Hodja attempted to sell his donkey. However, his donkey possessed a rather cantankerous temperament, kicking those who dared to examine its tail and biting anyone who dared to inspect its teeth. The commotion caused quite a stir, drawing the attention of onlookers and the bazaar's crier.

With an exasperated sigh, the crier approached Hodja, his voice filled with frustration. "Hodja, it seems nobody is willing to buy your donkey. Its unruly behaviour has scared away potential buyers."

Rather than expressing disappointment or frustration, Hodja's face lit up with a triumphant smile. He responded to the crier's statement, revealing a surprising motive behind his actions.

"Well, my dear crier," Hodja declared, his voice laced with a hint of mischief. You see, I brought my donkey to the bazaar not with the intention of selling it but to let people truly understand the hardships I endure."

The bazaar transformed into a stage for empathy and understanding in that moment. The crowd's laughter transformed into nods of acknowledgement and a newfound appreciation for Hodja's perseverance.

The story's moral is that sometimes, unconventional actions or seemingly negative situations can serve a purpose beyond what meets the eye. Nasreddin Hodja's antics with the unruly donkey were not aimed at selling the animal but rather at fostering empathy and understanding among the people in the bazaar. It highlights that there may be hidden motives or lessons in our actions and that perspective and understanding can turn challenges into opportunities for connection and appreciation.

# The Criticism of Men

Nasreddin Hodja, accompanied by his son, embarked on a trip to the market. Opting for a more leisurely journey, he positioned his son comfortably on a donkey and walked alongside him.

As they meandered through the village, a passerby couldn't resist commenting, "Nowadays, young people have their old fathers walking while they enjoy the comfort of a donkey."

Upon hearing this, the son, displaying remarkable compassion, promptly dismounted and insisted that his father take the donkey. Nasreddin Hodja, touched by his son's consideration, graciously accepted the gesture, and now, his son proceeded on foot.

Their journey continued, roles reversed, until another observer interjected, "Look, the big man is riding on a donkey, and the young boy is walking. Isn't that a pity?" Noting the observation, Nasreddin Hodja adapted once more. This time, he shouldered his son on his back.

Yet, as they progressed, a group of chatterboxes criticized, "But they are unjust people. Can two people ride a donkey? Poor donkey!" Growing frustrated, Nasreddin Hodja made a decisive move; he abandoned the donkey altogether. Together, they walked, leading the donkey in front of them.

Further along their journey, they encountered more onlookers who exclaimed, "Oh my God, what foolishness is this? Let the donkey go empty in front of them, and let them walk on foot in this heat, covered in sweat!"

With a sigh, Nasreddin Hodja came to terms with the realization that pleasing everyone was an impossible feat. Turning to his son, he shared a timeless lesson, "You see, son, if there's anything you can't escape, it's the opinions of people. Let love guide you. Do what you believe is right, no matter what the world says. The mouths of people are not like bags where you can silence them." And so, guided by the wisdom of Nasreddin Hodja, they continued their journey through the bustling market.

The narrative of Nasreddin Hodja and the donkey serves as a metaphor for the challenges of navigating societal expectations and the impossibility of pleasing everyone. It encourages individuals to stay true to their values, act with compassion, and not be swayed by the constant and often conflicting opinions of others. Nasreddin Hodja's wisdom imparts a valuable lesson about the importance of self-authenticity and the understanding that external judgments should not dictate one's path in life.

# Heavy Coat

One fateful night, a cacophonous commotion echoed from Nasreddin Hodja's humble abode, alarming the townsfolk. Curiosity piqued, they eagerly sought an explanation for the unsettling sound that had disturbed their peace. As the morning sun cast its warm glow upon the village, they approached Hodja with inquisitive gazes, eager to unravel the mystery.

With a mischievous smile, Hodja calmly responded to their inquiries, "Oh, that noise? It was merely my coat falling downstairs."

Baffled, the townspeople couldn't fathom how a simple coat could produce such a thunderous clamor. They questioned Hodja, their voices laced with scepticism, "Can a coat make such a noise?"

Undeterred by their scepticism, Hodja, ever the master of wit, replied with a hint of amusement, "If you were in it, like me, yes!"

With his clever retort, Hodja skilfully invited the townsfolk to look beyond the surface and consider the broader context. He encouraged them to understand that it was not the coat itself that caused the noise, but rather the weight and presence of a person within it. The humorous twist highlighted the importance of perspective and personal experience in shaping one's perception of events.

In essence, Hodja's response served as a gentle reminder to suspend judgment and embrace empathy. By inviting the townspeople to imagine themselves in his shoes, or rather his heavy coat, he encouraged them to consider alternative viewpoints and to approach situations with a deeper understanding.

# The Day of Judgement

In the vibrant city, a man approached Nasreddin Hodja, acknowledging his reputation as a wise and learned individual. Filled with curiosity, the man inquired, "Hodja, can you enlighten me on when the Day of Judgement will arrive?"

Nasreddin Hodja, renowned for his quick wit and insightful responses, offered a gentle smile and replied, "The Day of Judgement will come the day after you die," a response tailored to the man's character.

Perplexed by this unexpected answer, the man sought further clarification. "How can you possibly know that?" he asked, eager to understand the reasoning behind Nasreddin Hodja's statement.

With a glint of humour, Nasreddin Hodja responded, "My dear sir, it is because that is the day when the quarrels over your inheritance will turn the world upside down."

The man paused, struck by the truth of Nasreddin Hodja's words. He realized that conflicts and disputes arising from inheritance can lead to upheaval and turmoil among family members. Nasreddin Hodja's response, although playful, offered a profound perspective on human interactions and the potential consequences of unresolved conflicts.

Enlightened by Nasreddin Hodja's wisdom, the man actively embraced the importance of harmony, understanding, and love, prioritizing these values over material possessions. This proactive approach led him to mend relationships and foster goodwill among his loved ones, recognizing that proper judgment is reflected in navigating conflicts and interactions on Earth. Nasreddin Hodja's words sparked a positive transformation,

highlighting the enduring power of wisdom in shaping a
peaceful and balanced life.

# Dream

One night, Nasreddin Hodja found himself in a dream, a realm where generous souls bestowed nine gleaming gold coins upon him. Yet, in this ethereal slumber, Hodja's desire for even greater abundance took hold, yearning for a tenth coin to complete the fulfilment of his dream.

In a bold display of conviction, Hodja promptly declined the offer of the nine gold coins, driven by his unwavering aspiration for more. But as the dream dissipated and reality slowly unveiled itself, he awoke to find his hands empty. Regret washed over him as he realized that his opportunity for wealth had slipped through his grasp.

Swiftly, Hodja closed his eyes again, returning to the dream realm, hoping to recapture what had seemingly slipped away. With an air of resignation, he quietly whispered, "It's okay, I'll take the nine coins."

Reflecting on this peculiar dream, Nasreddin Hodja shared his experience with a friend, who listened intently. Hodja explained, "You know, in the dream, I wanted that tenth coin so badly, thinking it would complete everything. I turned down nine excellent coins to pursue something more."

His friend chuckled, "Well, dreams can be tricky, Hodja. What happened next?"

With a thoughtful expression, Hodja continued, "Upon waking up, I realized my hands were empty. I regretted chasing that elusive tenth coin. So, I closed my eyes, hoping to go back and accept what I initially dismissed."

His friend nodded, understanding dawning on him. "So, did you get the tenth coin in the end?"

Hodja smiled wryly, "No, my friend. I whispered, 'It's okay, I'll take the nine coins.' Sometimes, what we seek in pursuit of perfection blinds us to the blessings already around us."

His friend chuckled, "A valuable lesson from the dream realm, Hodja. Perhaps it's a reminder to appreciate what we have in the waking world."

In a world driven by aspirations for more, Hodja's dream invites us to pause and reflect on the importance of appreciating what is already within our grasp. It teaches us that true contentment lies not in ceaseless acquisition but in recognizing and valuing the blessings in our lives.

# Hodja's Writing

In a humorous encounter, an acquaintance approached Nasreddin Hodja, requesting him to write a letter to a friend in Khotan. Without hesitation, Hodja agreed, stating, "I will write any letter you want, but I can't go to Khotan these days."

Perplexed, his acquaintance responded, "Oh Hodja, I think you misunderstood. I didn't want you to go to Khotan. I said to write a letter."

To this, Nasreddin Hodja wittily replied, "I write, but my writing is not legible. I must go to Khotan to read the letter. It's better to have the letter written by someone whose writing is legible!"

In this humorous tale, Nasreddin Hodja, with his amusing antics, playfully claims that his handwriting is so unique that only he can read it, necessitating his presence in Khotan to interpret the letter. The story serves as a light-hearted commentary on the complexities of communication and the humour that can emerge from misunderstandings, showcasing Hodja's clever and amusing nature.

# Drink the Lake Baghrash[4]

In the lively city of Korla[5], a crafty merchant concocted a scheme to entertain and test the gullibility of the townsfolk. He enlisted the town crier to make a grand announcement, proclaiming that a reward of one thousand Yarmaq [6] awaited anyone who could drink the vast expanse of Lake Baghrash dry.

Nasreddin Hodja, renowned quick thinking, caught wind of this proclamation and saw an opportunity for amusement. With a mischievous glint, he boldly declared his intention to drink Lake Baghrash dry.

News spread rapidly, and on the appointed day, a curious crowd gathered at the designated location, eager to witness this seemingly impossible feat. Excitement filled the air as people anticipated the spectacle.

Confidently, Nasreddin Hodja said, "I am ready." The merchant, caught off guard but determined to uphold his promise, agreed to proceed.

However, Nasreddin Hodja, always the clever trickster, had his own condition. Slyly, he suggested, "Before we begin, dear merchant, you must stop the rivers from flowing into Lake Baghrash. Otherwise, the water will continue to replenish itself, and I will never be able to drink it all."

In shock, the merchant retorted, "How can I stop rivers from flowing into the lake?"

"If you can't stop the river from flowing into the lake, how could I empty Lake Baghrash?" Hodja replied.

---

[4] freshwater lake on the northeastern rim of the Tarim Basin.

[5] Korla is the second largest city by population in Uyghur Region.

[6] Yarmaq was name for Uyghur currency before.

Realizing the impracticality of the task he had set, the merchant acknowledged his defeat. It was impossible to halt the mighty rivers from replenishing the lake, making the challenge insurmountable.

The merchant willingly accepted his defeat and handed Nasreddin Hodja the promised one thousand Yarmaq. The crowd, thoroughly amused by Hodja's cleverness, erupted in laughter and applause.

This tale underscores the importance of discernment, critical thinking, and not falling prey to empty promises or impossible tasks. Nasreddin Hodja's witty response and clever twist exposed the merchant's scheme, turning the tables and showcasing the value of a sharp intellect.

# Yawns and Witty Replies

In a lively conversation meeting attended by Nasreddin Hodja, a particularly talkative individual dominates the discussion, leaving no room for others to speak. This chatterbox incessantly goes on, addressing everyone from left to right, while Hodja, bored and disengaged, finds himself yawning repeatedly.

Once the conversation finally concludes, the talkative man, perhaps noticing Hodja's apparent silence, turns to him and remarks, "Well, Master, you never opened your mouth?" Anticipating another round of endless talking, Hodja offers a clever retort.

"Mr, how did I not open my mouth? My jaw almost split in half from yawning," Hodja quips, using humour to convey both his weariness with the lengthy discourse and a play on the idea of "opening one's mouth." This short anecdote captures Nasreddin Hodja's penchant for witty responses, even in situations where words alone might not suffice.

# If I knew

One day, someone mysteriously stole Nasreddin Hodja's cherished donkey, his invaluable companion for various tasks. With the donkey gone, Hodja found himself in a predicament, unable to complete essential work that relied on his faithful animal.

Frustrated and disheartened, Hodja shared his woes with a friend, expressing the difficulty of navigating life without his indispensable donkey. As he aired his grievances, nosy neighbours couldn't resist prying into his misfortune, bombarding him with unnecessary questions.

Inquiring minds pressed on:

"What's wrong, Hodja? Did they steal your donkey?"

"Hodja, do you know who stole it?"

"When was your donkey stolen?"

Overwhelmed and irritated by the relentless questioning, Hodja reached his breaking point and responded emphatically:

"Hey, neighbours! Would I ever have had the donkey stolen if I knew who?"

In this humorous retort, Nasreddin Hodja cleverly highlights the absurdity of the neighbours' questions, pointing out the obvious – if he had known who stole his donkey, he wouldn't be facing the predicament in the first place. The tale offers a playful commentary on the tendency of people to state the obvious or ask unnecessary questions in times of distress.

# Miracle of Turban

One day, while Nasreddin Hodja was engaged in lively conversation with his friends in the mosque courtyard, a stranger approached, holding a letter. Unknown to Hodja, the man handed him the letter and politely requested, "Sir, please read this letter."

Always ready for a witty response, Hodja took a moment to inspect the letter and then declared, "This letter is written in Persian." Realizing the language barrier, he advised the man, "Son, I can't read this letter. You should find someone else who can."

Somewhat puzzled, the man persisted, "Sir, why don't you read my letter?" He became more insistent and questioned, "Why can't you read it?"

With his characteristic humour, Hodja replied, "Son, I don't know Persian, so I can't read it." Displeased with this response, the persistent man retorted, "You wear your turban and robe, and you can't read the letter. Is that possible?"

Though visibly annoyed, Hodja maintained his composure, mindful of his position. As the man continued his tirade, Nasreddin Hodja decided he had had enough. Rising from his seat, he asserted, "If knowledge is in the robe and the turban, go ahead and read it yourself." With a theatrical flair, he placed his robe and turban in front of the man, humorously challenging the idea that one's attire determines one's abilities.

In this amusing encounter, Nasreddin Hodja uses his quick wit to playfully dismantle the notion that clothing, or appearance correlates with knowledge. The tale reflects Hodja's ability to navigate absurd situations with humour and a touch of sarcasm.

# My Business' and Your Business

As Nasreddin Hodja headed home after the evening prayer, he encountered a chatty man who eagerly shared some gossip:

"Sir, they were just taking a roast goose from here."

Hodja, indifferent to the affairs of others, responded, "It is none of my business if they took a roast goose."

The man insisted, "But sir, the roast goose was going to your house."

This revelation did little to change Hodja's disposition. Annoyed, he retorted, "Mr, then it is none of your business, is it?" Hodja scolded the man, emphasizing that even if the matter involved his household, it was still not the concern of the chatty passerby.

By employing this humorous exchange, the story gently reminds us that we should not meddle in other people's affairs or become overly concerned with matters that do not affect us directly. It serves as a light-hearted lesson in minding our own business and not unnecessarily involving ourselves in the affairs of others.

# Challenging Uyghur language

In the vibrant city where Nasreddin Hodja resided, a foreigner arrived with a keen interest in learning the Uyghur language. Intrigued by its unique sounds and cultural richness, the foreigner sought guidance from the renowned Hodja.

Expressing his frustrations, the foreigner approached Nasreddin Hodja with a sigh and said, "Hodja, I find the Uyghur language incredibly challenging to learn. It seems to elude my grasp at every turn."

Nasreddin Hodja chuckled, and replied, "Dear traveller, our language is not as difficult as it may initially appear. Even our children effortlessly speak it."

Perplexed, the foreigner wondered how children could so effortlessly acquire something that he deemed challenging. Seeking further clarification, he asked, "But Hodja, how can children effortlessly speak the Uyghur language while I find it so challenging?"

With a warm smile, Nasreddin Hodja shared a valuable insight, "You see, dear friend, children possess a remarkable quality—they approach learning with curiosity, fearlessness, and a willingness to embrace the unknown. They absorb the language naturally, without the weight of self-doubt or judgment. They listen, imitate, and effortlessly navigate the intricacies of communication."

He continued, "To truly learn and embrace a language, we must shed our inhibitions, open our hearts and minds, and adopt the innocence and openness of a child. We must be willing to make mistakes, to stumble upon unfamiliar sounds and structures, and to persist despite the challenges. When we do so, we unlock the beauty and simplicity within the language."

The foreigner's eyes widened as he grasped the more profound meaning within Nasreddin Hodja's words. It was not merely about mastering grammar or vocabulary; it was about embracing the essence and spirit of the language, immersing oneself in its culture, and embracing the childlike wonder of learning.

Inspired by Nasreddin Hodja's wisdom, the foreigner embraced language learning with renewed enthusiasm, letting go of his fear of mistakes and finding joy in discovery. Through diligent practice and an open, childlike curiosity, he gradually immersed himself in the Uyghur language and culture, forming deep and meaningful connections with the community. His journey became a timeless reminder that even the most challenging endeavours can be overcome with curiosity, perseverance, and a willingness to learn from every experience.

# To Face Mecca

As Nasreddin Hodja strolled through the bustling marketplace, a man approached him with a sincere question, "In which direction should I turn to face Mecca?" Aware of the prevalent presence of thieves in the market, Nasreddin responded with a witty and practical answer.

Observing the surroundings and realizing the potential danger, Nasreddin replied, "The direction in which your bags are." In this clever response, Nasreddin Hodja cleverly redirected the man's attention to the practical matter of safeguarding his belongings, highlighting the importance of personal safety and security in a potentially hazardous environment.

In this story, Nasreddin Hodja emphasizes the importance of prioritization and practicality. He advises a man to protect his belongings in a market known for thieves, rather than solely concentrating on facing Mecca for prayer. Hodja's clever response highlights the need to assess immediate concerns and make pragmatic choices, while also stressing the importance of balancing spiritual observance with everyday responsibilities. The tale reminds us to remain vigilant, prioritize well-being, and integrate spirituality into daily life while making sensible decisions that align with our values and circumstances, creating a harmonious balance in our lives.

# Tit for Tat

In this amusing tale, Nasreddin Hodja was engrossed in repairing the roof when a man called out from below.

Curious, Hodja asked, "What do you want?"

The man replied, "Come down for just a minute. I'll tell you something!"

Intrigued, Nasreddin Hodja descended from the roof, and the man quickly said, "Can you lend me some money?"

With a sly smile, Hodja responded, "Come up above for just a minute."

The man followed him onto the roof. When surveying the surroundings, Nasreddin Hodja said, "I have no money!"

This witty exchange showcases Nasreddin Hodja's cleverness and ability to navigate tricky situations with humour. The Hodja turned the tables on the man, inviting him to the roof, where he cleverly revealed his lack of funds. This unexpected response surprised the requester, highlighting Hodja's knack for humorously addressing situations. In this brief yet witty exchange, Nasreddin Hodja finds himself in a classic "tit for tat" situation, demonstrating his quick thinking and clever approach to social interactions.

# The Hardest and the Easiest

Once, Nasreddin Hodja found himself in a bustling market square, surrounded by eager listeners who admired his wisdom and wit. A young student approached him with a curious question.

"Teacher," the student asked, "what is the hardest thing and what is the easiest thing in the world?"

Nasreddin Hodja smiled, recognizing the opportunity to impart a valuable lesson. He paused for a moment, letting the question hang in the air, before responding with a twinkle in his eye.

"The most difficult thing," he said, "is to know oneself."

The student was puzzled. "But why, teacher?" he asked, his curiosity piqued.

Nasreddin Hodja leaned closer, his voice filled with gentle sincerity. "You see, my young friend," he began, "knowing oneself is a lifelong journey. It requires deep introspection, self-reflection, and a willingness to confront one's fears, weaknesses, and strengths. It means peering into the depths of your soul, acknowledging your flaws, and embracing your true essence. Only through this profound self-awareness can we truly understand our purpose and navigate the complexities of life."

The student nodded; his gaze fixed on the wise teacher. Nasreddin Hodja continued, "On the other hand, giving advice to others is the easiest thing."

The student was puzzled once again. "But why is that so, teacher? Aren't guiding others a responsible and challenging task?"

Nasreddin Hodja chuckled softly. "Indeed, guiding others is a noble undertaking," he replied. "However, it often requires less self-reflection and introspection than knowing oneself. When we offer advice to others, we observe their situations from an outside perspective, drawing upon our knowledge and experiences. It is simpler to analyse someone else's predicament objectively and provide guidance without the burden of personal biases or emotions."

"But," Nasreddin Hodja added, a mischievous grin forming on his lips, "it is vital to remember that advice should always be given with humility, empathy, and an understanding that each person's journey is unique. It is easy to offer solutions, but true wisdom lies in recognizing that sometimes, the best course of action is to simply listen, support, and encourage others to find their own paths."

The student nodded, his mind buzzing with newfound insights. Nasreddin Hodja's words resonated deeply within him, planting seeds of self-reflection and empathy.

# It does not fill the empty belly

In the humble abode of Nasreddin Hodja, hunger gnawed at his stomach, and he longed for a satisfying meal. Seeking nourishment, he turned to his wife and pleaded, "Please, my dear, prepare something for me to eat. I can no longer bear the pangs of hunger."

His wife, engrossed in her prayers, replied with a serene smile, "Be patient, my love. Look at how beautifully I am engaged in my prayers. Once I have completed my devotion, you can satiate your hunger."

With a mischievous twinkle in his eyes, Nasreddin Hodja gently retorted, "Ah, my dear wife, the beauty of your prayers may uplift the soul, but it does not fill the empty belly."

Startled by his response, his wife paused and realized the truth within his words. Deep inside, she knew that spiritual devotion, while significant, could not quell the physical needs of her hungry husband.

This exchange between Nasreddin Hodja and his wife offers a profound lesson on balancing priorities. It highlights that while spiritual pursuits are essential, attending to basic human needs is equally vital. Nasreddin Hodja's gentle reminder to his wife emphasizes the necessity of addressing practical concerns even during spiritual devotion. The story is a timeless reminder of the delicate balance between spiritual growth and fulfilling everyday necessities, leading to a more balanced and enriched life.

# Where should we go

In the quaint village where Nasreddin Hodja resided, a day unfolded with an encounter that would showcase the Hodja's wit and wisdom. A mischievous relative, harbouring a desire to taunt him, approached Nasreddin with a question that lingered in the corridors of his mind.

"Sir," the relative began with a smirk, "we all know that one day, we'll meet our inevitable fate. Death is certain, no doubt about it. But there's one thing I've always wondered about: Where should we go with the coffin after the funeral prayer is performed?"

Nasreddin Hodja, ever quick-witted and undeterred by the attempt to harass him, pondered the question. With a sly grin, he offered a response that reflected his unique perspective on life and death.

"Well," he quipped, "as long as you do not go in the coffin, it does not matter wherever you go."

The Hodja's retort, laden with subtle humour and a touch of philosophical insight, left the relative momentarily stunned. Nasreddin Hodja's ability to turn even the trickiest of questions into a lesson in perspective became a hallmark of his teachings

# Hodja's Lost Donkey.

One day, Nasreddin Hodja found himself facing an unexpected challenge - his donkey had gone missing. The news quickly spread, and concerned villagers gathered around Hodja, their minds buzzing with questions and curiosity.

"Why did you lose it?"

"Why didn't you secure the stable more firmly?"

"You should have slept more alertly!"

"Why didn't you lock the door of the stable?"

"How can you be so careless?"

The barrage of questions echoed through the village, each villager offering their own piece of advice on how Hodja could have prevented the loss of his donkey. Some suggested stronger stable measures, while others questioned the Hodja's attentiveness.

During the inquiry, Hodja, with an air of calm and a hint of amusement, acknowledged their concerns. He listened to their suggestions about fortifying the stable with stronger measures and nodded thoughtfully.

"Why didn't you bolt the stable door or build higher walls to prevent theft?" a villager pressed.

With a touch of sarcasm and self-awareness, Hodja replied, "Yes, you're right. It's my fault, of course, not the thief's."

The villagers were initially surprised by Nasreddin Hodja's witty response to the loss of his donkey, finding humour in blaming him rather than the true culprit. As the story spread, it became a profound lesson in humility, resilience, and the importance of facing challenges with a constructive attitude. The revised moral emphasizes the value of taking responsibility and offering help in difficult situations rather than engaging in blame. Hodja's approach encourages us to acknowledge our role in outcomes, foster resilience, and focus on productive actions rather than unhelpful questioning.

# Weight of Head

Once, Nasreddin Hodja was visiting Khotan and engaged in a peculiar conversation with a man notorious for asking silly questions. On this day, the man approached Hodja with a curious inquiry, having learned that Nasreddin Khodja was in Khotan.

"Hey Hodja, how much does a person's head weigh?" asked the man, with a twinkle of mischief in his eyes.

Hodja immediately identified the man as garrulous at first glance and responded with a deadpan expression, "Well, it should be around fifteen pounds."

Not catching the sarcasm, the man questioned further, "I do not believe that."

Seizing the opportunity to infuse a lesson into the conversation, Hodja playfully suggested, "If you don't believe, what do you think if we cut off your head and weigh it?"

The man was left in contemplation after Hodja's unexpected response. With a subtle smile, Hodja continued, "You see, my friend, some things are better believed than tested. We do not need to verify the weight of a person's head through such extreme measures."

When the Khotanese overheard Nasreddin Hodja's witty response to the man's silly question, they were entertained by its clever moral lesson. The story spread, emphasizing the importance of trust and the potential pitfalls of unnecessary scepticism. Hodja's humorous reply, delivered with a twinkle in his eye, reminds us to accept credible information without always demanding impractical proof, encouraging a balanced approach to curiosity. The tale underscores the value of trust and warns against excessive doubt that can lead to absurd or harmful actions.

# Whom Do You Believe

In this amusing story, the Hodja finds himself in a situation where he is caught in a lie. When his friend asks to borrow his donkey, the Hodja tries to avoid lending it by claiming that he has already lent it to someone else. However, the donkey's loud braying from the stable exposes his deceit.

One day, a close friend of Hodja approached him with a humble request. The friend needed a donkey to make a two-hour journey to the market, and he thought Hodja's donkey would be perfect for the task. Hodja, however, was fond of his donkey and hesitant to lend it away.

Seeking a way to politely refuse, Hodja concocted a clever response. He turned to his friend and said with a smile, "Dear friend, I would love to lend you my donkey, but I have sent it to the mill. You see, it is grinding away, working hard."

The friend, a bit disappointed but understanding, prepared to leave for the market on foot. As he was about to take his first step, a peculiar sound filled the air. It was the unmistakable braying of a donkey, coming from Hodja's own house. Surprised and confused, the friend turned back to Hodja, his face expressing a mix of surprise and indignation.

"Hodja!" the friend exclaimed, "I thought you said your donkey was at the mill. But here I hear it, loud and clear!"

Hodja, maintaining his calm demeanour, replied with a twinkle in his eye, "Dear friend, tell me, who do you choose to believe? The braying of a donkey or a man adorned with white hair and a weathered beard?"

Faced with the evidence of his lie, the friend accuses the Hodja of cheating him. In response, the Hodja cleverly turns the situation around and questions the friend's judgment. He sarcastically asks the friend whom he believes—the Hodja, a human being capable of deceit, or the donkey, an animal incapable of speaking or understanding human language.

This story showcases the Hodja's sharp wit and ability to think on his feet, using humour to defuse tension and playfully challenge the friend's accusation.

# The Battle of Wits

Once, in a distant land, there lived three wise men who travelled far and wide in search of knowledge and understanding. They were known for their sharp intellect and their thirst for wisdom. One day, they arrived in the town of Kashgar and sought an audience with the governor, requesting the presence of the most learned man in the district. The governor obliged and summoned Nasreddin Hodja, the renowned sage of Kashgar, to meet the three wise men in the bustling marketplace.

As the crowd gathered, the three wise men decided to test Hodja's wit before engaging in discussions. The first wise man approached Hodja and posed a perplexing question: "Could you tell us the exact location of the centre of the world?" Hodja, without hesitation, responded, "Yes, I can. It is just under the left hind leg of my donkey." The wise man, intrigued but skeptical, demanded proof. Hodja calmly replied, "If you doubt my word, you are welcome to measure and see."

Perplexed and unable to refute Hodja's answer, the first wise man withdrew. Emboldened, the second wise man stepped forward and presented his question: "Can you tell us how many stars there are in the sky?" Hodja, quick-witted as ever, retorted, "As many as the hairs on my donkey's back." The wise man challenged Hodja, seeking evidence to support his statement. Unfazed, Hodja responded, "If you doubt my word, you are welcome to count them all and find out." The wise man, realizing the impossibility of such a task, fell silent.

Seeing his companions' failed attempts, the third wise man approached Hodja, filled with sarcasm. He taunted Hodja, saying, "Since you seem so well acquainted with your donkey, can you tell us how many hairs there are on the tail of the beast?" Hodja, maintaining his calm demeanour, replied, "Certainly, as many as the hairs in your beard." The wise man challenged Hodja to prove his claim. Without hesitation, Hodja proposed a simple experiment: "I will pull one hair from your beard, and you will pull one out of my donkey's tail. If both do not finish at the same time, then I will admit that I have been mistaken."

Realizing the absurdity of the situation, the third wise man wisely chose not to proceed with the experiment. In that moment, all three wise men recognized the greatness of Hodja's wisdom. They understood that his quick thinking, sharp wit, and ability to turn their challenges into clever responses were a testament to his profound understanding of the world.

The battle of wits in Kashgar taught everyone presents a valuable lesson. It reminded them that true wisdom goes beyond knowledge and facts. It encompasses the ability to think creatively, find unconventional solutions, and gracefully navigate intellectual challenges. Nasreddin Hodja, with his wit and humour, became a symbol of wisdom that transcended mere intelligence.

# Walnuts and Pumpkins

Nasreddin Hodja found himself pondering the wisdom of Allah/God while resting under a walnut tree. As he marvelled at the tree's strength and grandeur, he questioned why such a mighty tree would bear only small walnuts as its fruit. In contrast, he wondered why pumpkins, which grow on fragile vines, produced such large and heavy fruit.

Lost in his thoughts, Hodja drifted off to sleep. Suddenly, he was jolted awake by a walnut falling from the tree and striking him on the forehead. Surprised but unharmed, Hodja exclaimed, " The Creator be praised!" In that moment, he realized the profound wisdom behind the natural order of things.

Hodja recognized that if the world had been created according to his limited understanding, it would have been a heavy pumpkin falling from the tree, which surely would have caused harm or even death. Through this humbling experience, he acknowledged the greater wisdom and foresight of The Creator. Hodja's initial questioning and subsequent encounter with the falling walnut served as a reminder of the limitations of human wisdom and the intricate design of the natural world.

Filled with gratitude and awe, Hodja exclaimed, "The Creator be praised! The Creator is most wise!" He embraced the realization that the world, with all its intricacies and seeming imperfections, is a testament to the wisdom and perfection of its Creator.

From that day forward, Nasreddin Hodja carried this lesson in his heart, humbly accepting the natural order of things and recognizing that true wisdom lies in embracing the wisdom of The Creator, even when it goes against our own limited understanding. The story of Hodja and the falling walnut became a cherished tale, teaching others the importance of humility, gratitude, and acknowledging the greater wisdom that lies beyond human comprehension.

# Most Dangerous Creature

In a moment of contemplation, Nasreddin Hodja was posed with a question about the most dangerous creature in the world. Without hesitation, he replied, "Humankind." Perplexed by his response, those around him sought an explanation for his statement.

Nasreddin began to unravel the essence of his answer. He explained, "A dog remains faithful to the one who feeds it. A wolf avoids the path that a human has traversed. Even a snake will not cause harm if left undisturbed. But is this the nature of mankind?"

With his words, Nasreddin drew attention to the complexities and potential dangers that lie within human nature. He contrasted the loyalty of a dog, the instinct of a wolf, and the neutrality of a snake with the intricate and unpredictable behaviours exhibited by humans.

The moral of the story is that Nasreddin Hodja's assertion that "humankind" is the most dangerous creature underscores the complexities and potential dangers within human nature. By contrasting the behaviours of animals with the unpredictable actions of humans, Nasreddin prompts reflection on the multifaceted nature of human behaviour. The story encourages genuine acts of kindness, emphasizing their intrinsic value over expectations of reciprocation. Nasreddin's words serve as a cautionary tale, urging conscious navigation of human nature and highlighting the power individuals must shape positive interactions. Ultimately, the story encourages the cultivation of compassion, empathy, and gratitude for their inherent value in making a positive difference in the world.

# Everyone Is Right

In a small town where Nasreddin Hodja served as a *qadi*[7], a dispute arose between two neighbours. Seeking justice, the first neighbour approached the Hodja with a complaint against the other. Attentively, the Hodja listened to the charges and, after thoughtful consideration, responded, "Yes, dear neighbour, you are quite right."

Shortly after, the second neighbour came forward to present their defence. With the same level of attention, the Hodja listened to their side of the story and concluded, "Yes, dear neighbour, you are quite right."

Observing the entire proceeding, the Hodja's wife couldn't help but intervene. She remarked, "Husband, both men cannot be right. Their accounts contradict each other."

The Hodja replied to his wife, "Yes, dear wife, you are quite right."

Nasreddin Hodja conveyed a profound message about the subjective nature of truth and perspective through this simple exchange. Each neighbour saw themselves as right based on their own experiences, and rather than passing judgment, Hodja acknowledged the validity of both viewpoints. His response, a testament to his wisdom, highlights that reality is often shaped by individual perceptions and biases, reminding us that truth is multifaceted. The tale underscores the importance of understanding and empathy in resolving conflicts and seeking justice. Hodja's approach, a beacon of wisdom, exemplifies his ability to navigate delicate situations with humour and wisdom, encouraging introspection and mutual understanding.

---

[7] a judge

# Allah's House

One day, a beggar approached Nasreddin Hodja's house and confidently declared, "Allah has directed me to this house for a good meal."

Hodja "I am sorry, my friend, but you seem to have made a mistake. Allah's house is not here."

Perplexed, the beggar looked around, trying to make sense of Hodja's statement. Pointing towards a nearby mosque, Hodja continued, "If you seek the benevolence of Allah, His house is over there."

The beggar, realizing his error, thanked Hodja for his guidance and made his way towards the mosque to seek the blessings of Allah through the generosity of the people gathered there.

The tale underscores Nasreddin Hodja's wisdom in redirecting a beggar to the mosque for help, emphasizing the significance of communal spaces in seeking divine blessings. Hodja subtly promotes the importance of community, shared values, and collective responsibility in assisting those in need. The story showcases his understanding of religious customs and his humorous yet insightful approach to guiding others toward appropriate channels for seeking divine support.

# The Lost Donkey

Despite losing his donkey and embarking on a search to locate it, he is seen smiling throughout the ordeal. When someone questions his unusual behaviour, he provides a clever and thought-provoking response.

Nasreddin explains, "Well, I'm lucky. If I had been riding my donkey, I'd be lost as well." This witty remark carries a deeper meaning and offers a valuable lesson about perspective and gratitude.

The story of Nasreddin Hodja losing his donkey and responding with a smile imparts a valuable lesson about perspective and gratitude. Nasreddin's witty remark on being lucky not to be riding the donkey at the time carries a deeper meaning, urging us to reflect on attachment and the consequences of relying too heavily on external possessions. The tale encourages cultivating a positive outlook, finding gratitude in challenging situations, and embracing life's unpredictability. Nasreddin teaches that true resilience and contentment come from detaching ourselves from material possessions and appreciating the present moment.

# Witness

In a bustling town, where justice was sought and truth was revered, an intriguing court case unfolded. Nasreddin Hodja found himself entangled in an unusual predicament. An acquaintance, desperate for a favourable outcome, beseeched Hodja to testify falsely on his behalf. Initially hesitant, Hodja reluctantly agreed to support him in court.

The day of the trial arrived, and the courtroom was filled with anticipation. Hodja's acquaintance confidently presented his case, accusing the defendant of owing him two sacks of wheat. The judge, known as *qadi*, turned to Hodja, the chosen witness, to offer his account.

Taking a deep breath, Hodja began his testimony, veering away from the truth. "Yes, Mr *Qadi*," he spoke, "the defendant owes two sacks of oat to the plaintiff." The words hung in the air, causing a momentary pause among the onlookers.

The plaintiff, sensing the falsehood in Hodja's statement, quickly interjected, seeking to rectify the miscommunication. "Mr *Qadi*, the Hodja misspoke. He meant to say wheat, not oat."

In that crucial moment, Hodja's wisdom shone through as he responded with a poignant remark. "What difference does it make if it's oat or wheat, so long as it's a lie!"

Silence enveloped the courtroom, and the weight of Hodja's words settled upon everyone present. In that simple statement, Hodja unveiled a profound truth about honesty and integrity. He highlighted the fundamental principle that a lie, regardless of its content, is still a betrayal of truth.

The room erupted in contemplative murmurs, as the people recognized the profound wisdom in Hodja's words. The judge, Mr *Qadi*, reflected on the essence of justice and the importance of upholding truthfulness in all matters.

Ultimately, the case took a different turn. The truth began to unravel, and the deceitful intentions of Hodja's acquaintance were exposed. The court recognized Hodja's integrity and the power of his words, and justice was served.

This story serves as a timeless reminder that truth is an unwavering beacon, and honesty should be our guiding principle in all aspects of life. In the face of temptation and pressure, Nasreddin Hodja's wisdom prevails, inspiring us to stay true to ourselves and to embrace the path of truth, even when it seems easier to choose falsehood.

# Miser

In the ancient city of Kashgar, there lived a notorious miser known far and wide for his stinginess. He would clutch onto every coin with a firm grip, rarely parting with anything, not even a smile. The people of the town often whispered about his selfish ways, but they never imagined that one day, his greed would lead him to a perilous situation.

On a fateful day, as the sunbathed the town in its golden hues, the miser found himself standing at the edge of a riverbank. Perhaps driven by his curiosity, or perhaps lost in his own thoughts of accumulating wealth, he took one step too far and tumbled into the rushing waters. Panic quickly took hold of him as he realized he couldn't swim.

The villagers, sensing danger, rushed to the riverbank, calling out to him, "Give me your hand! We will save you!" Their voices blended into a chorus of urgency, pleading for his safety. However, the miser remained stubborn, refusing to extend his hand to anyone.

Just as hope seemed to slip away, Nasreddin Hodja, the wise and quick-witted figure of the town, happened to pass by. The good Samaritans quickly informed him of the miser's predicament, their voices filled with worry and frustration.

Hodja, ever ready to find a solution, approached the river's edge. With a commanding voice, he called out to the miser, "Sir. Sir! Take my hand!" In that moment, the miser, driven by his instinct to grasp onto anything that could benefit him, reached out and firmly grasped Hodja's outstretched arm.

With the strength of the villagers and the assistance of the Hodja, the miser was pulled from the treacherous waters, saved from the clutches of the river that nearly claimed his life.

As the miser stood on the riverbank, coughing, and catching his breath, the Hodja turned to the gathered crowd and offered his insight with a knowing smile. "You see," he explained, "this man's stinginess runs so deep that he has become more adept at taking than giving."

The crowd in Kashgar recognized the profound truth in Nasreddin Hodja's words, leading the miser to learn a valuable lesson about the joy and fulfilment that comes from giving. The story of the miser serves as a timeless reminder that true wealth is found not in material possessions but in the generosity of the heart. Hodja's intervention, a catalyst for change, reveals the miser's deep-seated stinginess, prompting a transformative realization about the importance of helping others. The tale encourages embracing generosity and compassion, highlighting that life's true fulfilment comes from sharing and supporting those in need.

# Pot

During his travels, Nasreddin Hodja arrived at a village to take some rest. As he mingled with the villagers, they couldn't help but boast about their recent harvest.

"You won't believe it, Mr Hodja," they exclaimed, "this year we had a bumper harvest of pumpkins. They are as big as a donkey cart!"

Hodja, always quick with his wit, decided to play along with their enthusiasm. He responded, "Ah, that's quite impressive! In our city, the craftsmen are incredibly skilled as well. They have been busy making a pot as big as a small house!"

The villagers, intrigued yet puzzled, questioned Hodja's statement. "How is that possible? How can a pot be as big as a small house? It doesn't make sense!"

With a mischievous smile, Hodja replied, "Well, my friends, if there were not such a colossal pot, how would you cook your enormous pumpkins? You see, it takes a pot that big to accommodate such large pumpkins!"

Nasreddin Hodja's witty response to the villagers' boasting about their oversized pumpkins left them momentarily speechless as they realized the humour in his logic. The story highlights the importance of balancing pride with practicality, as Hodja playfully points out the need for an enormous pot to cook such giant pumpkins. This clever twist not only encourages the villagers to think beyond their initial excitement but also enlightens them about the practical implications of their achievements. The tale serves as a reminder to approach accomplishments with perspective and critical thinking, promoting a balanced and realistic approach to success.

# Basket

One day, a neighbour approached Nasreddin Hodja's door with a request to borrow a basket. However, Hodja had an interesting response to the neighbour's seemingly simple request.

"I'm sorry, my dear friend, but we cannot lend you our basket," Hodja replied with a mischievous smile, "because we have put some water in it."

Perplexed, the neighbour couldn't help but question Hodja's response. "Why would anyone ever put water in a basket?" he asked, his disbelief evident.

Hodja, still smiling, gave a witty answer that carried a deeper meaning. "You see, my friend," he said, "sometimes people put water in a basket when they simply don't want to lend it."

Nasreddin Hodja's seemingly absurd response about water in the basket cleverly conveys a more profound lesson about setting boundaries and declining requests. Using a humorous and unconventional excuse, Hodja not only illustrates a polite way to say no without directly refusing, but also adds an element of entertainment to the lesson. The story highlights how people often use creative explanations to avoid fulfilling requests, underscoring the importance of respecting personal boundaries. Hodja's approach promotes understanding and open-mindedness in the art of refusal, encouraging a light-hearted and respectful way to handle such situations..

# Appreciation

In the town where Nasreddin Hodja resided, his wisdom and charisma drew people from far and wide to hear his sermons. One day, as he stood before the congregation, he posed a thought-provoking question that echoed through the hallowed halls.

"My friends," Nasreddin began, his voice carrying a sense of solemnity, "a day will come when I will no longer walk among you, and you will be asked how you knew me in my mortal form. What will be your response?"

The congregation pondered his words, reflecting on the impact Nasreddin had made on their lives. They spoke in unison, "We will say that we knew him to be a good man, wise and compassionate."

A mischievous glint danced in Nasreddin's eyes as he responded, "Ah, my dear friends, if that is truly how you perceive me, then why wait until I have departed this earthly realm? Why not let me hear those words of appreciation now?"

Nasreddin Hodja's words left the congregation in reflective silence as they grasped the truth in his simple yet profound message. The story underscores the importance of expressing admiration and gratitude while people are still present, emphasizing that such words are most valuable when spoken to the living. Hodja's thought-provoking question about how they would talk about him after his departure prompts the community to appreciate and uplift one another in the present. This tale serves as a reminder to regularly express love and admiration, fostering a culture of warmth and appreciation that brings joy and nourishment to those around us, enriching our lives and theirs.

# End of The World

In the village, there were some mischievous youths who learned that Nasreddin Hodja owned sheep. They devised a plan to play a prank on Hodja and enjoy a feast by eating his sheep.

One day, they approached Hodja and said, "Dear Hodja, tomorrow is the Day of Judgment, the end of the world. What's the point of keeping your sheep? Let's eat it today by the riverside."

Hodja, always known for his wit, responded, "If the end of the world is truly upon us, then I agree. What's the point of keeping my sheep? Help yourselves."

Excitedly, the mischievous youths rushed to the riverside and swiftly slaughtered the sheep. While waiting for the meat to cook, they decided to go for a swim in the river, taking off their coats and leaving them by the water's edge.

Meanwhile, Hodja calmly built a fire, placed a pan over it, and began preparing the meal. However, instead of attending to their coats, Hodja carefully collected and piled them onto the fire, watching as they burned to ashes.

When the mischievous youths returned to enjoy their meal, they were shocked to find their clothes missing. They turned to Hodja, pleading, "Hodja, please give us back our clothes. This is no time for jokes."

Hodja, maintaining his composure, responded, "No joke, my friends. I burned your clothes."

Confused and alarmed, the youths asked, "But what will we wear now?"

Hodja replied with a hint of irony, "Why worry about clothes when tomorrow is supposedly the end of the world? What's the point of keeping them?"

The mischievous youths in the village learned a valuable lesson from Nasreddin Hodja's clever response. Hodja's witty actions highlighted the folly of their prank and conveyed a deeper message about the transient nature of material possessions. By burning their clothes in the face of the supposed end of the world, Hodja humorously illustrated the insignificance of worldly belongings. The story encourages reflection on the priorities that truly matter in life and serves as a reminder not to get caught up in trivial pursuits or attachments. Hodja's ironic approach challenges us to focus on what brings genuine meaning and value to our lives, especially when confronted with the impermanence of our existence.

# How can one become wise?

In the realm of wisdom and knowledge, Nasreddin Hodja was known for his insightful words. One day, a curious individual approached him, seeking guidance on how to attain wisdom.

"How can one become wise?" the person asked with genuine interest.

Nasreddin Hodja smiled and replied, his voice filled with wisdom, "To become wise, one must learn the art of listening."

Perplexed, the individual inquired, "But what do you mean, Hodja? How does listening lead to wisdom?"

Nasreddin Hodja gently explained, "When you encounter a wise person speaking, lend them your ears. Pay attention to their words, for in their wisdom lies profound knowledge and guidance. Open your mind and heart to truly hear what they have to say. By attentively listening to the wisdom of others, you open yourself up to new perspectives, insights, and a wealth of knowledge that can shape your understanding of the world."

The individual nodded, taking in Nasreddin Hodja's words. Sensing their curiosity, Nasreddin Hodja continued, "But remember, listening is not only about external voices. It is equally important to listen to yourself when you speak."

Puzzled, the person asked, "Listen to myself? But why, Hodja? I already know what I am saying."

Nasreddin Hodja smiled warmly, "Indeed, you may think you know what you are saying, but true wisdom comes from self-reflection. When you speak, listen to your own words with attention and introspection. Reflect on the thoughts and beliefs you express and question their validity. By listening to yourself, you can uncover your own biases, learn from your mistakes, and grow in understanding."

He continued, "To become wise, one must embrace the duality of listening: lending ears to others and listening to oneself. Through this delicate balance, you gain the wisdom of the collective and the wisdom within yourself, fostering personal growth and a deeper connection with the world around you."

The individual nodded, grateful for Nasreddin Hodja's guidance. They understood that wisdom was not solely acquired through external sources but also through deep self-reflection and the ability to truly listen to the voices within and around them.

From that moment on, the person made a conscious effort to listen carefully, to take in the wisdom of others, and to pay close attention to their own words. Through this practice, they embarked on a journey towards true wisdom, ever seeking knowledge and understanding, both from the world and from within themselves.

# Need

One day, the king approached Nasreddin Hodja and posed a thought-provoking question, "Hodja, if you had to choose between money and justice, which would you choose?"

Without hesitation, Hodja responded, "Money."

The king was taken aback by Hodja's answer and exclaimed, "What? I would choose justice. Money, after all, is not rare. Contrarily, justice is very rare in this world."

Hodja calmly replied, "Your Majesty, it is human nature to always want what they do not have. We often desire the things that seem elusive or scarce to us. In your case, money is something that you already possess and experience within your realm. Therefore, it is only natural that you value and prioritize justice over money. On the other hand, since I have never possessed an abundance of wealth, I am inclined to choose money."

The story of Nasreddin Hodja's response to the king's question serves as a reminder of the subjective nature of desires and priorities. Hodja's witty answer challenges the king's perspective on justice and money, highlighting the influence of individual experiences and circumstances on personal choices. The tale encourages reflection on our biases and the importance of considering diverse viewpoints. It prompts the king to approach situations with justice and empathy, recognizing that what may seem abundant to some might be scarce to others. Ultimately, the story invites us to cultivate open-mindedness and understanding in our interactions with others, fostering a more inclusive and compassionate outlook.

# Question

Indeed, one day a man approached Nasreddin Hodja and notice his way of responding to questions.

"Hodja," the man said, "I've noticed that you have a habit of answering every question with another question."

Hodja, with a mischievous smile, replied, "Do I?"

Nasreddin Hodja's habit of responding with a question enlightens us about the persistence of habitual activities. The playful exchange with the man underscores the idea that ingrained habits and behaviours don't change overnight. Hodja's mischievous response, "Do I?" serves as a reminder that patterns of communication and behaviour are deeply rooted and may require time and conscious effort to transform.

# Vizier and Donkey

In the kingdom of wisdom, there lived a wise and fair king who valued intelligence and integrity above all. Hodja had a special bond with his donkey, whom he believed to be incredibly intelligent.

One day, while Hodja was conversing with the townspeople in the bustling market square, he made a bold statement. "My donkey is more intelligent than the vizier of the king!" he proclaimed with a mischievous smile. The words spread like wildfire and reached the ears of the vizier himself.

Feeling insulted and threatened, the vizier wasted no time and reported Hodja's audacious claim to the king. The king, intrigued by the notion, summoned Hodja to the palace for an explanation.

In the grand hall, surrounded by courtiers and advisors, the king questioned Hodja about his seemingly outrageous statement. Hodja, undeterred by the intense atmosphere, calmly presented his proof.

"Your Majesty, I have witnessed the intelligence of my donkey firsthand," Hodja began. He recounted the incident on the wooden bridge, describing how his donkey had managed to free its foot from a hole and thereafter carefully avoided it on subsequent crossings.

Hodja continued, his voice filled with conviction. "On the other hand, Your Majesty, the vizier has been caught stealing from the treasury multiple times, despite facing severe consequences. If he possessed even a fraction of my donkey's intelligence, he would have learned from his mistakes and refrained from such actions."

The king, deeply reflecting on Nasreddin Hodja's words, came to the profound realization that accurate intelligence involves learning, adapting, and making wise choices rather than mere knowledge or status. Addressing the vizier, he noted that intelligence is shown through actions and growth, using Hodja's donkey's cautious behaviour as an example. The king then appointed a new vizier from his advisers, emphasizing the need for wisdom and self-improvement. The story highlights that wisdom goes beyond knowledge, stressing the importance of learning from mistakes and making better choices, and demonstrates that valuable insights can come from unexpected sources.

# Sleep and Thirst

Once, Nasreddin Hodja embarked on a journey from Kashgar to Aqsu[8]. Along the way, he found himself in a village where a hospitable villager graciously offered him shelter for the night.

As the evening approached, the generous host, eager to attend to Hodja's needs, asked, "Hodja, are you sleepy or thirsty?"

Notably, the man omitted any mention of food, a detail that did not escape Hodja's discerning gaze. Unfazed by the absence of a dinner invitation, Hodja responded with his characteristic wit and humility, "I had a good sleep by the Chaqmaq River[9] on my way here."

The moral of the story is that Hodja demonstrates the art of graceful and indirect communication. Rather than outright rejecting his friend's offer of sleep and water, Hodja subtly expresses his need for sustenance by sharing a story about having slept by the river. Through his clever and indirect request, Hodja navigates the situation with tact and humour, emphasizing the importance of effective communication and consideration for others' feelings. The story encourages us to be mindful of how we convey our needs and desires, promoting diplomacy and understanding in our interactions.

---

[8] A city along the Taklamakan Desert
[9] A river between Kashgar and Atush City

# Wall

Hodja, observing the construction workers diligently building the wall of the magistrate court, couldn't help but be curious about their efforts. Intrigued, he approached them and inquired about their task.

"What are you doing?" he asked with genuine curiosity, his eyes scanning the rising wall.

A worker, pausing for a moment to catch his breath, replied, "We are building the wall higher to prevent thieves from entering the magistrate court. With a taller wall, we hope to keep the valuable items and documents safe."

Hodja's face brightened with a mischievous grin as he pondered their response. After a brief pause, he offered his own perspective.

"No use," Hodja chuckled, "the main thief is already inside the wall. How can this high wall stop them?"

The workers exchanged puzzled glances, unsure of Hodja's intentions or the meaning behind his words.

Hodja continued, his voice filled with wisdom, "You see, a wall can only keep out those who are outside. But the real threat lies within, hidden among those trusted and given access. It is not the height of the wall that truly safeguards the treasures, but the integrity and honesty of those within."

The moral of the story is that true security and protection come not only from physical barriers but also from fostering an environment built on principles of integrity, trust, and virtuous conduct. Hodja's wisdom highlights the importance of focusing on internal factors, such as the character and honesty of individuals within an organization, rather than relying solely on external defences like high walls. The story encourages us to prioritize ethical practices, accountability, and transparency, recognizing that these elements contribute significantly to a secure and trustworthy environment.

# Chicken or Egg

In the realm of philosophical inquiries, Nasreddin Hodja found himself confronted with the timeless question that had puzzled minds for ages: "Did the chicken come from the egg, or did the egg come from the chicken?"

As the curious question was posed to him, Nasreddin, always wise and profound, offered an answer that transcended the boundaries of mere biology and ventured into the realm of spirituality.

With a gentle smile, Nasreddin responded, "Neither. Whatever comes, comes from Almighty God."

The moral of the story is that Nasreddin Hodja's response emphasizes a perspective that transcends the debate of whether the chicken or the egg came first. Instead of delving into a scientific or biological explanation, Hodja's answer introduces a spiritual dimension. It suggests a humility and acknowledgment of a higher power, attributing the origin of all things to the divine. The story encourages contemplation on broader, philosophical aspects of existence, highlighting the mystery and awe of creation beyond the scope of human understanding.

Hodja, enjoying a moment of relaxation near the tranquil lake, was approached by a curious passerby. The passerby, seeking wisdom, posed a question to Hodja.

"Hodja, if you are a wise man, tell me, how many buckets of water are in this lake?"

Hodja smiled, and replied, "It depends on the size of the bucket."

Perplexed, the passerby questioned, "What do you mean by that?"

Hodja explained, "You see, my friend, the number of buckets of water in this lake is relative to the size of the bucket. If the bucket is as big as the lake itself, then there is only one bucket of water in the lake. However, if the bucket is half the size of the lake, then there would be two buckets of water in the lake."

The passerby pondered Hodja's answer, realizing the deeper meaning behind his words. It wasn't just a matter of counting the amount of water in the lake; it was a reflection on the perspective from which we view things.

The moral of the story lies in Hodja's response, emphasizing the relativity of perspectives and the importance of considering context in our understanding of situations. It encourages us to be mindful of how our perception is influenced by the parameters we set and the perspectives we adopt. The story teaches the value of embracing diverse viewpoints and recognizing that there can be multiple valid ways to interpret a situation. In essence, it encourages open-mindedness, flexibility in thinking, and an appreciation for the complexity of perspectives that contribute to a more comprehensive understanding of the world.

# While We Are Chatting

As Hodja sold his honey in the bustling market, a stingy man approached him with the intention of cheating him out of his goods. Hodja began pouring the honey into a bowl for the man, but the man, being his stingy self, started asking numerous questions and attempted to leave without paying a single yarmaq.

Not willing to let the man get away with his deceitful tactics, Hodja confronted him, "Sir, you haven't paid for the honey."

The man, trying to come up with an excuse, replied, "I thought I paid while we were chatting."

Hodja, unyielding and quick-witted, took the bowl of honey and poured it back into the honey bucket. With a clever smile, he retorted, "Well then, if you thought you ate the honey, you can go now."

The moral of the story lies in Hodja's commitment to honesty, fairness, and accountability. The tale emphasizes the importance of standing up for what is right and not allowing deceit or unfair practices to go unaddressed. Hodja's clever response serves as a reminder that actions speak louder than words, and it encourages us to be vigilant against dishonesty while finding creative and intelligent ways to uphold our principles. Ultimately, the story promotes values of integrity and fairness in our interactions with others.

# Good Health

In the realm of desires and material possessions, Nasreddin Hodja was once confronted with a thought-provoking question: "Oh Hodja, which would you prefer—a magnificent horse, a splendid house, or a hundred glittering gold coins?"

To the surprise of those who posed the question, Nasreddin responded with utmost simplicity and wisdom. He said, "None of them. All I want is good health."

The moral of the story lies in Nasreddin Hodja's wise choice and emphasis on good health over material possessions. It encourages us to prioritize and appreciate the value of our physical and mental well-being above the pursuit of external wealth or luxuries. Nasreddin's simple yet profound response serves as a reminder to focus on the foundation of a fulfilling life – good health – and to make choices that nurture and prioritize our well-being in a world that often places emphasis on material possessions.

Once, Hodja made a light-hearted remark to one of the king's generals, saying, "You will die in two days." However, by a twist of fate, the general tragically fell from his horse and passed away exactly two days later. When the king learned of this, he was filled with anger and sought to punish Hodja for his seemingly prophetic words. He commanded his soldiers to bring Hodja to the palace for questioning.

Upon meeting with the king, Hodja was confronted with the accusation of being responsible for the general's death. The king questioned him sternly, "Hodja, you are accountable for the death of my general. You claim to have known the day of his demise, but do you also know when you are going to die?"

Maintaining his composure, Hodja calmly replied, "Yes, Your Majesty. Yesterday, as I contemplated the mysteries of the stars, they revealed to me that I would meet my end two days prior to your own passing."

Nasreddin Hodja's witty response, delivered with a playful irony that is sure to entertain, cleverly deflects blame and addresses a potentially dangerous accusation. By claiming he would meet his end two days before the king's demise, Hodja maintains his innocence while subtly questioning the validity of the prophecy about the general. This humorous retort underscores the power of words and perspective, illustrating how the interpretation of statements can shape their perceived meaning. The story, while light-hearted, conveys a more profound message about the limitations of human knowledge and the unpredictable nature of fate, encouraging reflection on life's complexities and inherent uncertainties.

# Soup of the soup

A few people from a neighbouring village, who were acquaintances of Nasreddin Hodja, visited him in the city and presented him with a hare as a gesture of respect. Hodja warmly welcomed his guests and invited them to stay for dinner. His wife skilfully prepared the hare, and they all enjoyed a delicious meal together.

A few days later, there was a knock on Hodja's door once again. This time, unfamiliar faces greeted him, introducing themselves as the relatives of the individuals who had brought him the hare. Hodja, upholding the Uyghur tradition of hospitality, graciously welcomed them into his home. His wife prepared a hearty soup for dinner, and Hodja proudly declared, "It is the soup of the hare."

As fate would have it, a couple of days later, another group of strangers arrived at Hodja's doorstep. They explained that they hailed from the neighbouring village of the people who had initially presented Hodja with the hare. Although Hodja was surprised by the unexpected visit, he had no choice but to extend his hospitality once more. However, this time he had a playful response to the situation.

When it was time for dinner, Hodja brought a large pot filled with clear well water to the table. The bewildered guests questioned Hodja about the contents of the pot, expressing their disappointment. With a hint of jest in his voice, Hodja replied, "It is the soup of the soup of the hare."

This humorous tale illustrates Hodja's wit and cleverness in light-hearted situations. It also reflects the cultural value placed on hospitality and generosity in Uyghur traditions. Despite the unexpected and continuous visits from unfamiliar guests, Hodja and his wife graciously welcomed them into their home and shared what they had. The final twist with the "soup of the soup of the hare" adds a playful touch, highlighting Hodja's humorous response to the repetitive nature of the circumstances.

Overall, the story serves as a reminder of the importance of hospitality, even in unexpected situations. It showcases Hodja's quick thinking and ability to find humour in everyday occurrences, leaving a lasting impression on those who hear the tale.

# Word- Challenges of Communication

In a moment of contemplation, someone approached Nasreddin Hodja and posed a thought-provoking question: "Hodja, what's the hardest thing in the world?" Nasreddin, known for his insightful and enigmatic responses, provided a profound answer that touched upon the complexities of communication.

With a touch of wisdom, Nasreddin replied, "The hardest thing in the world is a word, hard to explain and hard to understand."

The moral of the story is to emphasize the inherent challenges of communication and the limitations of language. Nasreddin Hodja's insight encourages humility, patience, and a willingness to understand others by acknowledging the complexities of conveying and comprehending words. The story advocates for active listening, seeking clarification, and embracing diverse perspectives to foster empathy and bridge gaps in understanding. It highlights the importance of approaching conversations with clarity and compassion, recognizing that while words can be powerful tools for connection, they also have the potential for misunderstanding and miscommunication.

# I Am Sleeping

One day, Hodja and his friend travelled to a town and decided to spend the night at a caravanserai. As the night grew darker, Hodja's friend suddenly woke him up from his slumber.

"Hodja, are you sleeping?" his friend asked.

Startled by the interruption, Hodja replied, "What happened?"

"Well," his friend continued, "can you lend me some money?"

Without missing a beat, Hodja responded with a mischievous grin, "I am sleeping."

In this playful exchange, Nasreddin Hodja uses his wit to handle an unexpected and amusingly bizarre request with humour. Instead of a direct refusal or lengthy discussion, Hodja cleverly cites being woken up as a reason to avoid the request altogether, adding a humorous twist to the situation. This anecdote serves as a reminder to approach life's interruptions with a sense of humour and to find joy in unexpected moments. Hodja's quick-witted response brings a smile and highlights his creative approach to everyday challenges.

# More Often

In a moment of illness and vulnerability, Nasreddin Hodja found himself visited by concerned individuals who sought to provide comfort. They reassured him, "Don't be anxious or afraid, Hodja. In this world, death comes only once."

Nasreddin He weakly lifted his head and shared a perspective that carried a deeper meaning. He said, "That's what I'm afraid of. If death came more often, I wouldn't be worrying."

The story is to encourage a deeper understanding of life's impermanence and inspire individuals to embrace each moment fully. Nasreddin Hodja's perspective on the fear of death highlights the paradoxical nature of human emotions surrounding mortality. By expressing a longing for death to be a more common event, he prompts reflection on the anxiety that stems from the perceived finality and uncertainty of life. The story encourages us to confront our fears, appreciate the fleeting nature of existence, and make the most of our time by cherishing meaningful experiences and relationships. Ultimately, Nasreddin's contemplation invites us to live authentically and with a profound appreciation for the preciousness of life.

# Gratitude, the Advice of Hodja

One day, a man who had heard about Hodja's wisdom and insight sought his advice. He approached Hodja with a question that had been weighing on his mind.

"Dear Hodja," the man began, "I have witnessed many things in this world, and I find myself unsure of what I should remember. Can you offer me some guidance?"

Hodja, without a pause for a moment, answered the man's question. He shared his profound advice.

"In this world," Hodja said, "if someone else has done something good for you, it is important to remember it and hold it close to your heart. But if you have done something good for someone else, you can simply let it go and forget about it."

Reflecting on Nasreddin Hodja's advice, the man appreciated the practicality of gratitude and humility. Hodja's words emphasized the importance of appreciating the kindness of others and letting go of one's deeds. True selflessness, Hodja suggested, is about performing good acts without expecting anything in return. This practical wisdom empowers us to embrace gratitude, acknowledge the interconnectedness of human relationships, and adopt a humble mindset that focuses on the positive actions of others rather than our own acts of goodness.

# Ask Him

As Hodja made his way to the market, a curious crowd halted his progress, eager to gain his insights on the mysteries of the afterlife.

"Hodja, can you tell us what the next world is like after we die?" they inquired with anticipation.

Hodja paused for a moment, contemplating the question. His eyes caught sight of a funeral procession passing by a sombre reminder of the transient nature of life.

"Ask the man inside the coffin," Hodja replied, gesturing towards the procession. "For he is on the journey to the next world as we speak."

The crowd fell silent, captivated by the solemnity of Nasreddin Hodja's response, which invited deep introspection about the mysteries of the afterlife. Hodja's words, imbued with humility and reverence, urged the crowd to focus on the impermanence of life and find meaning in the present moment rather than speculating about what lies beyond. As the crowd dispersed, they were left in deep contemplation about their mortality and the choices they make. At the same time, Hodja's simple wisdom reminded them of the importance of cherishing the present and finding meaning in their current lives.

# Falling Tales

One day, Nasreddin Hodja found himself in a rather precarious situation while working on the roof of his house. A sudden mishap occurred, and Hodja, much to the concern of his neighbours, took an unintended descent to the ground. The news quickly spread through the village, and concerned neighbours rushed to express their well-wishes and inquire about the incident.

"Sir, get well soon! We heard you fell off the roof, and we're very sorry," they exclaimed in a chorus of sympathy. However, their genuine concern soon gave way to a barrage of questions.

"How did it happen?"

"Why weren't you more careful?"

"Please be more cautious next time..."

As the stream of questions flowed, Nasreddin Hodja, starting to feel a tinge of boredom, decided it was time to put an end to the inquisition. With a thoughtful expression, he interrupted the well-meaning neighbours.

"Neighbours," he began, "has any of you ever fallen off a roof?" The neighbours exchanged puzzled glances and responded in unison, "Nooooo..."

Nasreddin Hodja, seizing the moment to impart a lesson, grinned and replied, "Well, then don't talk in vain. Only those who have fallen from a roof will truly understand my situation!"

The Hodja's clever retort not only lightened the mood but also conveyed a valuable message about the limitations of understanding certain experiences without having lived through them. The neighbours, momentarily taken aback, couldn't help but appreciate the wisdom wrapped in Hodja's humorous response. And so, the tale of Nasreddin Hodja's rooftop misadventure and his witty comeback became another cherished story in the village, showcasing the Hodja's ability to turn everyday incidents into lessons in humour and insight.

# Complexities of Human Relationships.

In a moment of casual inquiry, a well-wisher approached Nasreddin Hodja and asked, "Hodja, how are you?" Nasreddin, known for his wit and clever responses, offered a nuanced answer that reflected the complexities of human relationships.

With a hint of humour and wisdom, Nasreddin replied, "If you're asking me as an enemy, the answer is I'm fine. But if you're asking as a friend, it's a long story."

The story is to emphasize the complexities of human relationships and the nuanced dynamics between individuals. Nasreddin Hodja's witty response to "How are you?" reveals the layers of understanding and intentions inherent in human interactions. The story encourages us to be mindful of the different dimensions of relationships, acknowledging that the same question may elicit varied responses based on the nature of the connection. Nasreddin's insights prompt us to reflect on the significance of genuine friendship, highlighting the need for time, trust, and shared experiences to build deep and meaningful connections. Ultimately, the story encourages us to approach relationships with discernment, understanding, and a willingness to invest in the richness of human connection.

# Best Music

Hodja's friend, a lover of music, had invited him over for lunch. As Hodja entered his friend's home, he was greeted with an array of musical instruments on display. His friend proudly showcased his collection, playing a few tunes to demonstrate their melodic capabilities.

As time went on, Hodja couldn't help but notice that despite the musical extravaganza, there was no sign of lunch being prepared. The focus seemed solely on the instruments, leaving Hodja with an empty stomach and a curious mind.

Finally, his friend posed a question, asking Hodja to choose between the sounds of the Dutar[10] and the Tembur[11], two of the instruments he had played earlier.

Hodja smiled and replied, "My dear friend, let me be honest with you. At this very moment, there is no sound more beautiful in the world than the gentle scrape of a spoon against a soup bowl."

Nasreddin Hodja's unexpected response to his friend, who was engrossed in music, served as a gentle reminder to appreciate life's simplest pleasures. While his friend had been focused on the grandeur of music, Hodja highlighted the joy found in ordinary moments, such as enjoying a nourishing meal. The sound of a spoon scraping against a bowl symbolised nourishment, warmth, and shared experiences. Setting aside their instruments, they prepared and savoured the meal together, fostering a sense of community and connection. Hodja's lesson emphasizes the importance of balancing grand experiences with the

---

[10] An ancient instrument from the family of tanburs, widely distributed among Uyghur.

[11] The tembur is a long-necked lute used in the music of Uyghur.

appreciation of everyday rituals, encouraging us to find joy
and gratitude in the simple moments that enrich our lives.

# Proud Mountain

One day, Hodja found himself in a boastful mood, proclaiming that he possessed the power to do anything he desired. Intrigued by his claim, the people around him decided to put him to the test. They challenged him to call upon the mighty mountain and bring it to them.

Eager to prove himself, Hodja stood before the grandeur of the mountain and called out, "Mr. Mountain, would you kindly come here for just a minute?" To the disappointment of the onlookers, nothing happened. Undeterred, Hodja repeated his call, hoping for a different outcome. Yet, the mountain remained steadfast and unmoving.

Realizing that his initial approach had failed, Hodja pondered his next move. After a moment of contemplation, he smiled and decided to take matters into his own hands. With a determined spirit, he began to walk towards the mountain.

Perplexed, one of the men questioned Hodja, "Where are you going? The mountain did not heed your call."

Hodja, with a gleam in his eyes, replied, "I, my friend, am not a vain person. If I call upon the mountain and it refuses to come to me, then I shall go to the mountain."

Hodja emphasizes the importance of humility, adaptability, and perseverance in the face of challenges. Nasreddin Hodja's initial claim to have the power to call the mountain serves as a setup for the lesson he imparts. When faced with the mountain's unresponsiveness, Hodja demonstrates true humility by not insisting on his original approach but instead adapting to the situation. The story teaches that genuine strength lies not in making grand claims but in recognizing our limitations, being flexible in our approach, and taking proactive steps towards our goals. Hodja's willingness to walk to the mountain illustrates the power of determination and resourcefulness, offering a valuable lesson in facing obstacles with a humble yet resolute mindset.

# The Ones Who Know

Nasreddin Hodja found himself in a peculiar situation with his group of followers. As he stood on his podium, ready to address them, he posed a question: "I have a few things I'd like to say to you, and I wonder if you knew what they were?"

In the first instance, the followers, unaware of what Hodja wanted to discuss, responded with a unified "No, we don't, dear Hodja." Perplexed by their lack of knowledge, Hodja humorously remarked, "Well, if you don't have a clue, what could I say to you?" He then dismounted the podium and returned home.

Undeterred by their initial response, Hodja tried again, asking the same question on a different occasion. This time, the followers, determined to outsmart him, confidently replied, "Yes, dear Hodja, we all know what you want to talk about." Seizing the opportunity, Hodja cunningly retorted, "Since you already knew, why should I tell you again?" and once again left the podium.

Finally, Hodja took another chance, mounting the podium for the third time. This time, the group responded with a more astute answer: "Dear Hodja, some of us know and some of us don't know what you meant to say." Pleased with their response, Hodja smiled, clapped his hands, and delivered his clever solution: "How nice! In that case, the ones who knew can tell it to the ones who didn't know."

The effective communication requires adaptability and awareness of your audience. Nasreddin Hodja's skilful navigation of his followers' responses underscores the importance of tailoring communication strategies. His insights highlight the limitations of speaking to those who don't understand, the necessity of preparation when addressing an informed audience, and the value of sharing knowledge within a community. The story encourages individuals to be mindful of the audience's comprehension level, to be well-prepared when engaging with knowledgeable individuals, and to actively contribute to the collective learning and growth of the community through the sharing of knowledge.

# Punch

In a bustling marketplace, Nasreddin Hodja found himself at the receiving end of an unexpected punch from a stranger. Startled and angered by the assault, the stranger quickly apologized, claiming that he had mistaken Hodja for someone else. However, Hodja, unsatisfied with the explanation, sought justice and demanded compensation for the offense.

Bringing the stranger before the Judge, Hodja anticipated a fair resolution. Yet, to his dismay, he soon realized that the Judge and the defendant were close friends, casting doubts on the impartiality of the proceedings. Despite the defendant admitting his guilt, Hodja's hope for a just outcome wavered.

To Hodja's surprise, the Judge pronounced an unusual sentence, stating that the settlement for the offense was one Yarmaq, a local currency, to be paid to the plaintiff. However, the Judge added that if the defendant did not possess a Yarmaq now, he could bring it to the plaintiff later.

Days turned into weeks, and the defendant failed to fulfil his obligation, leaving Hodja waiting in anticipation for the promised payment. Frustrated by the delay, Hodja approached the Judge once again, seeking clarification on the value of a Yarmaq in the context of the offense.

"Do I understand correctly that one Yarmaq is deemed sufficient payment for a punch?" Hodja inquired, his tone laced with scepticism.

The Judge, aware of the underlying irony in Hodja's question, replied with a simple affirmation, "Yes."

Hearing this response, Hodja seized the opportunity to highlight the absurdity of the situation. Without hesitation, he unleashed a punch of his own, striking the Judge in the face. With a mischievous grin, Hodja declared, "You may keep my Yarmaq when the defendant returns with it."

The story highlights the importance of standing up for justice, even in the face of adversity and apparent partiality. Nasreddin Hodja's shrewd actions underscore the significance of challenging authority and exposing inconsistencies. The tale emphasizes the need for justice to be blind and impartial, free from personal relationships or biases. Hodja's clever use of irony serves as a powerful reminder of the importance of holding those in positions of power accountable and striving for a fair and just society. The story encourages individuals to question authority, seek transparency, and work towards upholding the integrity of legal systems.

# The sheep and wolf

In a distant village, there lived a powerful official who was known for his ruthless and cunning nature. One day, as he was wandering through the wilderness, he stumbled upon a helpless sheep trapped in the clutches of a ferocious wolf. Acting swiftly, the official bravely intervened, saving the innocent creature from certain death.

Grateful for its rescue, the sheep felt obligated to follow its saviour back to his grand estate. The official, however, had ulterior motives that were far from noble. Upon reaching his home, he made a shocking decision—to slaughter the very sheep he had just saved. The innocent animal, sensing its impending doom, began to cry out in distress, its baa echoing through the air.

The commotion caught the attention of Nasreddin Hodja, a wise and compassionate neighbour known for his astute observations and insightful remarks. Curious about the uproar, Hodja hurriedly made his way to the official's residence to understand the cause of the sheep's anguish.

Upon arriving, Hodja saw the official holding the sheep, ready to carry out its fate. With a puzzled expression, Hodja questioned, "You see this sheep? You claim to have saved it from the jaws of a wolf, yet it seems to be cursing you. Why would this innocent creature accuse you of being a wolf yourself?"

Perplexed, the official responded, "Cursing me? What are you talking about?"

Hodja, with a knowing smile, explained, "It is not the sheep's literal words that accuse you, but rather the message behind its distress. The sheep symbolizes trust and gratitude, as it followed you willingly after you saved its life. However, in return for its trust, you chose to betray and harm it. Through its cries, the sheep reveals your true nature, highlighting that your actions are akin to those of a wolf in man's clothing."

The official, profoundly impacted by Nasreddin Hodja's words, realized the truth in them. Recognizing that he had misused his power to deceive and exploit those he was meant to protect, he was overcome with guilt and resolved to change his ways. The moral of the story, a profound lesson that our actions define our character and betraying trust has serious consequences, is one that should not be overlooked. Hodja's observation highlights the importance of integrity and empathy, showing how our choices reveal our true nature to those who trust us. The tale encourages reflection on the impact of our actions, promoting virtues like kindness and compassion over deception. It serves as a reminder to be worthy of the trust others place in us and to align our character with moral principles.

# Stick from Heaven

During a lively discussion on the topic of corporal punishment, Nasreddin Hodja found himself engaged in a debate. As someone expressed their support for the act of beating, they claimed, "The stick came from heaven, didn't it?"

Nasreddin responded with a thought-provoking rebuttal. He said, "If the stick had been a blessed thing, it would have stayed in heaven, not left it."

The story challenges the misguided notion that divine origin can justify violent actions, emphasizing that true blessings stem from compassionate and positive intentions. Nasreddin Hodja's witty response urges us to critically examine the morality of our actions and rethink what we consider 'blessed.' The tale reminds us of our responsibility to use our resources and abilities for the betterment of society, advocating for kindness, understanding, and non-violence as the authentic sources of blessings. Nasreddin's wisdom calls us to act with empathy and foster harmony in our interactions, highlighting that genuine blessings arise from compassion and, importantly, peaceful coexistence, offering a hopeful vision for the future.

# The Squeaky Shoe

One day, Hodja had a guest over at his house. As they were engaged in a conversation, the guest accidentally broke wind. To conceal the embarrassing sound, the guest quickly rubbed his shoe across the floor to create a similar noise.

Observing this, Hodja couldn't help but appreciate the guest's clever attempt to cover up the sound. With a mischievous smile, Hodja whispered, "You did well by covering up that sound with your squeaky shoe. But unfortunately, my friend, you did not manage to hide the smell."

The guest blushed, realizing that his effort to mask the sound had inadvertently drawn attention to the smell. However, instead of feeling embarrassed, he found himself laughing along with Hodja.

The story's moral is to embrace honesty and authenticity, recognizing that attempts to cover up mistakes or imperfections often lead to more awkward situations. Nasreddin Hodja's humorous tale illustrates the futility of trying to conceal the truth and highlights the importance of facing our flaws with humility. The story encourages individuals to be open about their mistakes, fostering genuine connections and understanding. By accepting our positive and negative aspects, we can create a more compassionate and authentic community. The laughter and camaraderie that follow in the tale serve as a reminder that moments of embarrassment can be transformed into opportunities for growth and connection through honesty and humility.

# The Significance of Always Telling the Truth

During one of his mentoring sessions with his students, Nasreddin Hodja imparted a valuable lesson about the importance of truthfulness. He emphasized the significance of always telling the truth, regardless of the potential consequences.

However, one student, perhaps influenced by his father's perspective, interrupted Nasreddin and expressed his concern. The student stated, "But my father says that if you tell the truth, you'll be expelled from nine villages.[12]"

Unperturbed, Nasreddin Hodja responded with unwavering conviction, "Take no notice. There's always a tenth village to be found."

It upholds the value of truthfulness, even in the face of potential challenges. Nasreddin Hodja's response highlights the importance of staying committed to honesty, regardless of the consequences, and emphasizes the long-term rewards of maintaining one's integrity. The tale encourages individuals to persevere in speaking the truth, even when it may seem difficult or unpopular, and to trust that staying true to one's principles will lead to new opportunities and stronger connections. Nasreddin's wisdom inspires a commitment to honesty as a guiding principle in life.

---

[12] The phrase "to be expelled from nine villages" is a Turkish idiomatic expression. It is used to convey that a person is not accepted in many places, is significantly socially excluded, or is widely rejected due to their violation of social norms and rules.

Not long ago, Hodja conversed profoundly with one of the respected Imams. The Imam, burdened by the constant demands and interruptions of countless individuals seeking his guidance daily, sought Hodja's counsel to find solace and make time for his spiritual practices.

"Dear Hodja," the Imam beseeched, "The world's weight seems to rest upon my shoulders as people flock to me incessantly, seeking answers and counsel. I yearn for a moment of tranquillity to devote myself to prayer. How can I free myself from this overwhelming burden?"

With compassion in his eyes, Hodja listened attentively to the Imam's plea. Contemplating the situation, he offered a solution that held profound wisdom within it. "Ask them for a loan, my revered Imam. And they shall not come near you again."

Perplexed by this unexpected response, the Imam inquired, "But why a loan, Hodja? How will that liberate me from this constant influx of people seeking my attention?"

With a gentle smile, Hodja began to elucidate the underlying wisdom hidden within his words. "O honourable Imam, when you ask for a loan, you subtly invite a shift in perspective. Any amount of loan should work. By suggesting this, I remind those who seek your counsel that only those with a genuine reason would present themselves; those who wanted to ask random questions will be afraid of your loan and should disperse."

He continued, "Even though you are going to return the loan you asked for when people understand that their requests carry weight and require a reciprocal loan, they become more conscious of their intentions. They begin to differentiate between genuine needs and trivial desires. In doing so, they learn to approach you with respect, consideration, and a sincere understanding of the preciousness of your time."

The Imam's face brightened as he grasped the profound wisdom within Hodja's response. He realized that the suggestion of a loan was not about rejecting or dismissing others but rather about fostering a reciprocal relationship based on respect and mindful consideration.

With renewed clarity and purpose, the Imam embraced Hodja's guidance. From that moment onward, when individuals approached him seeking guidance, he would ask for a loan. Most were surprised.

Word of the Imam's loan spread far; gradually, the number of visitors seeking the Imam's attention lessened. Those who remained approached him with a more profound understanding and reverence. The Imam found the time he desperately needed to nurture his spiritual practices and devote himself wholeheartedly to prayer.

The story teaches that by introducing a symbolic gesture like asking for a loan, one can foster respect and mindfulness in others, helping to distinguish genuine needs from trivial desires. It encourages thoughtfully setting boundaries to create a reciprocal relationship based on understanding and consideration.

# Loan and Time

In a typical encounter with his neighbour, Nasreddin Hodja was faced with a request from someone who had a habit of not repaying debts on time. Seeking financial assistance, the neighbour approached Nasreddin and asked, "I need a bit of money. Will you give me a time loan?"

Nasreddin responded with a clever retort. He said, "Look here, neighbour, you want not only a loan but time as well. I can't give you both at once. But I can give you as much time as you want."

The story revolves around the importance of valuing time as a precious resource, similar to money. Nasreddin Hodja cleverly uses humour to highlight the neighbour's habit of delaying payments and emphasizes the finite nature of time. The story encourages individuals to fulfil their obligations promptly, be accountable for their actions, and respect the time of others. It serves as a reminder to cultivate integrity, punctuality, and responsibility in order to build trust and maintain healthy relationships. Ultimately, Nasreddin Hodja's wisdom encourages a harmonious society where both time and money are valued and treated with consideration.

# Gratitude

Hodja found himself entangled in a peculiar situation. It all began when he was on the verge of falling into a pool, only to be rescued by a man he barely knew. Grateful for the assistance, Hodja expressed his thanks and thought nothing more of it.

However, the man who had come to his aid seemed to have a different perspective. Each time they crossed paths, he would bring up the incident and remind Hodja of the service he had performed. Initially, Hodja graciously acknowledged the man's help, but as the reminders persisted, it began to wear thin.

One day, when the man once again raised the subject, Hodja decided to address the situation head-on. He invited the man to the very edge of the pool where the incident had taken place. With a mischievous gleam in his eye, Hodja jumped into the water, submerging himself so that only his head remained above the surface.

From his watery perch, Hodja shouted to the man, "Now I am as wet as I would have been if you had not saved me! Leave me alone."

The man was stunned by Nasreddin Hodja's unexpected demonstration, through which Hodja imparted a profound lesson on the nature of obligations and gratitude. Hodja's clever act revealed that repeatedly reminding others of past favours can turn acts of kindness into burdensome obligations, diminishing their sincerity. The story's moral emphasizes the importance of selflessness in our acts of kindness and the liberating value of letting go of expectations. Hodja's playful yet insightful approach teaches that genuine gratitude should be heartfelt and free from any desire for leverage or control. The tale encourages us to appreciate the present, focus on the future, and perform kindness without expecting anything in return, highlighting the transformative power of genuine, unburdened gratitude.

# Secret of Longevity

As Hodja was known for his straightforward and succinct answers, he was approached one day by someone seeking the secret to longevity. The person was eager to discover the key to a long and healthy life. Hodja, never one to beat around the bush, shared his wisdom with a simple and concise response:

"Keep your feet warm, your head cool, be careful what you eat, and don't think too much."

At first glance, these words may appear simple, but they hold profound meaning and valuable advice for leading a long and fulfilling life. Let's delve into the wisdom behind Hodja's words.

"Keep your feet warm": This speaks to the importance of taking care of our physical bodies. Ensuring that our feet are warm signifies the need to prioritize our overall well-being. It reminds us to protect ourselves from the elements and maintain a healthy balance in our physical activities.

"Keep your head cool": Our minds are powerful, and maintaining a calm and composed state of mind is crucial for longevity. By keeping our heads cool, we emphasize the importance of managing stress, practicing mindfulness, and nurturing a peaceful mental state. This helps us maintain clarity, make better decisions, and handle life's challenges with grace.

"Be careful what you eat": Our dietary choices have a significant impact on our health and longevity. Hodja's advice highlights the importance of mindful eating and choosing nourishing foods. By being mindful of what we consume, we can provide our bodies with the nutrients they need to thrive, maintain a healthy weight, and prevent the onset of chronic illnesses.

"Don't think too much": This piece of wisdom reminds us of the importance of balance and not getting caught up in overthinking. Overthinking can lead to unnecessary stress, anxiety, and even hinder our ability to enjoy life. Hodja encourages us to find a balance between contemplation and action, to let go of excessive worry, and to embrace a more relaxed and light-hearted approach to life.

In essence, Hodja's advice on the secret to longevity is a gentle reminder to take care of ourselves holistically. By tending to our physical well-being, maintaining a calm mind, nourishing our bodies with wholesome foods, and avoiding excessive rumination, we can enhance our chances of living a long, healthy, and fulfilling life.

It is in the simplicity and practicality of Hodja's words that we find a profound truth. Longevity is not solely determined by external factors or complex regimens but by the mindful choices we make daily. By following these principles, we can embrace a balanced lifestyle that promotes longevity and well-being.

# Planting tree

One sunny day, as Hodja was planting young fruit tree saplings in his garden, a curious neighbour approached him with a hint of scepticism in his voice.

"When will these trees ' mature and give fruit?" the neighbour asked, a touch of doubt in his eyes. "You'll never get to eat that fruit."

Hodja paused for a moment, a mischievous smile playing on his lips. He looked at his neighbour and replied, "Of course, none of us will eat the fruit of these trees I'm planting. We eat the fruit of the trees the people before us planted. Let the next generation eat the fruit from our trees."

Perplexed, the neighbour pondered Hodja's words, trying to comprehend their deeper meaning. Sensing his neighbour's confusion, Hodja continued his tale.

"You see, my friend, life is a beautiful cycle. Just as we enjoy the fruits of the labour and wisdom of those who came before us, it is our duty to plant the seeds of hope and abundance for the generations yet to come. The trees we plant today may not bear fruit in our own hands, but they will provide nourishment and joy for our children, grandchildren, and beyond."

Hodja's words deeply impacted his neighbour, revealing that planting trees was an act of selflessness and care for future generations rather than mere personal gain. This revelation sparked a chain reaction of positive change. Inspired, the neighbour began planting his saplings, understanding that true fulfilment comes from leaving a lasting, positive legacy. The story of Hodja's wisdom spread throughout the village, motivating others to plant trees and sow seeds of love, knowledge, and kindness. As gardens bloomed and seasons passed, the villagers enjoyed the fruits of their labour, symbolizing hope and faith in the future. Hodja's tale teaches that the true purpose of life lies in selflessly nurturing the world for those who come after us, emphasizing the importance of leaving behind a legacy that benefits future generations.

# Advice

On a day when wisdom seekers gathered around Nasreddin Hodja, a profound question emerged from the crowd. They turned to him and asked, "Hodja, you possess unique insight. What is the most valuable thing in this world?"

Without hesitation, Nasreddin replied, "Advice."

Perplexed, the people inquired further, seeking an explanation for his choice. Nasreddin elucidated, "When advice is taken, it holds immeasurable worth, capable of transforming lives and guiding individuals towards prosperity. However, when advice is disregarded, it loses value, becoming as insignificant as a passing breeze."

According to Nasreddin Hodja, the most valuable thing in the world is advice. He emphasizes that its actual value lies in the willingness to listen, consider, and act upon the wisdom offered. The story highlights the transformative power of wise counsel in shaping decisions and destinies, underscoring the importance of humility, receptiveness, and the mutual relationship between those who give and receive advice. This mutual relationship creates a sense of community, where everyone is both a giver and a receiver of advice. When advice is taken to heart and applied, it becomes invaluable, leading to personal growth, deeper understanding, and positive change. Nasreddin's wisdom encourages us to appreciate the significance of advice, fostering a mindset of openness and discernment that unlocks the transformative power of guidance for meaningful growth.

# Fallen from a wall

In a bustling town, Nasreddin Hodja found himself in a rather embarrassing situation. He had fallen from a wall, and as he lay there, a concerned crowd quickly gathered around him, offering their assistance.

But instead of accepting their aid right away, Hodja calmly raised his hand and addressed the gathered crowd. "Please, let the person who fell from the wall before me come to help me," he said with a mischievous twinkle in his eyes. "Surely, they would know how to handle an injured man like me."

The onlookers were taken aback by Hodja's unexpected request. They exchanged puzzled glances, wondering if he had lost his senses. They had never encountered such a peculiar response to a simple offer of help.

After a moment of silence, a wise old man stepped forward from the crowd. He had a gentle smile on his face, having understood Hodja's underlying wisdom. The old man had indeed experienced a similar fall from the wall in the past and knew the challenges that came with such an incident.

"Very well, Hodja," the old man replied, extending a helping hand. "I have fallen from a wall before, and I understand the pain and confusion that accompanies such an accident. Let me assist you."

With the old man's guidance, Hodja was gently lifted to his feet, and the two walked together, supported by the collective strength and compassion of the crowd.

As they strolled away from the scene, Hodja turned to the old man, gratitude in his eyes. "Thank you for understanding the essence of my request," he said sincerely. "You see, my intention was not to mock the kind souls who offered help, but rather to remind everyone that those who have experienced similar hardships possess invaluable knowledge and empathy."

The old man nodded, his wise eyes sparkling. "Indeed, Hodja," he replied. "Life's challenges are not meant to be faced alone. By seeking the guidance and support of those who have walked a similar path, we can learn from their experiences, gain valuable insights, and find solace in the fact that we are not alone in our struggles."

From that day forward, Hodja's unique response became a cherished fable in the town, teaching the importance of seeking wisdom and guidance from those who have experienced similar trials. The townsfolk were reminded of the great value in connecting with others who have walked the path before them, as they possess the knowledge and, more importantly, the empathy needed to offer meaningful support. Hodja's words serve as a lasting reminder to embrace the wisdom of those who have faced challenges before us, finding strength, empathy, and valuable lessons to navigate life's difficulties with grace and resilience.

# Oleaster Seller

Once, in a bustling marketplace, Nasreddin Hodja found himself selling his delightful oleaster fruits. As he sat behind his stall, a half-acquaintance from a neighbouring community approached him with a curious expression.

"Sir, how's your oleaster?" the man inquired, his interest piqued by the mouthwatering display.

Hodja responded with a warm smile. "Taste it, sir," he said, offering a sample of the delicious fruit.

The man hesitated for a moment and then replied, "I've fasted."

Recognizing the man's observance of fasting, Hodja nodded understandingly.

"Oh, I see," Hodja said, acknowledging the man's commitment to fasting.

The man proposed, "Can I buy the Oleaster and give you the money later?"

Hodja, ever the clever one, responded with a mischievous smile. "Of course, you can," he said, allowing the man to believe he could make the purchase without immediate payment.

However, as Hodja handed over the Oleaster, a sudden realization struck him. This wasn't the holy month of Ramadan, a time traditionally associated with fasting.

Curiosity piqued, Hodja couldn't resist asking, "What are you fasting for?"

The man chuckled and replied, "I missed a couple of my fasting days during Ramadan three years ago, and now I'm making up for them."

Hodja, now fully aware of the situation, swiftly took back the Oleaster, reclaiming his produce.

"I'm sorry, but no, you cannot take it," Hodja firmly declared, a twinkle in his eye.

Confused, the man asked, "Why won't you give it to me now?"

Hodja's response was quick and clever. He asked, "If you can settle your debt to Allah in three years, then when do you think you can settle mine? "

Nasreddin Hodja's playful encounter with a man is a gentle reminder of the importance of integrity and responsibility. This lesson is not just for Hodja and the man, but for all of us. Through humour, Hodja emphasizes that true integrity lies in honouring commitments and repaying debts, regardless of circumstances. The story highlights the value of keeping one's word and fulfilling obligations, reminding us that excuses or delays do not diminish our duty to uphold our promises.

# Danger

Once, Nasreddin Hodja was riding his donkey through the village when a curious onlooker approached him with a question. "Hodja, why do you sit backwards on your donkey?" the villager asked, perplexed by Hodja's unconventional riding style.

Hodja offered a clever response. "I sit backwards on my donkey to see the danger from behind," he explained, emphasizing the importance of being aware of potential threats that may approach from behind.

Curiosity piqued, the villager continued, "But what if the danger appears in front of you?"

Hodja, with a mischievous twinkle in his eyes, delivered his final punchline. "Even the donkey can see the danger in front," he replied, implying that his donkey would react if a danger were to emerge from the front.

Nasreddin Hodja's unconventional way of sitting on his donkey serves as a humorous yet insightful lesson about being vigilant and aware of potential dangers. Hodja's clever response highlights the importance of considering all angles and being prepared for unexpected threats. The tale encourages a thoughtful approach to anticipating challenges, emphasizing the value of awareness and readiness in navigating life's uncertainties.

# Non-existent Colours and Non-existent Day

Hodja, the witty and resourceful man, decided to open a shop where he would colour clothes for people. One day, a curious customer walked into his shop with a unique request.

"Can you colour my cloth?" the customer asked, handing over the fabric to Hodja.

Hodja, always up for a challenge, smiled and replied, "Of course, but what colour would you like me to use?"

The customer grinned mischievously and said, "Colour it with a colour that doesn't exist in the world. No black, no yellow, no red, no blue, no green."

Hodja, unfazed by the unusual request, nodded and confidently said, "Okay, I can do that."

Intrigued, the customer asked, "When can I come to collect my cloth?"

Hodja, with a twinkle in his eye, replied, "Come to collect it on a day that doesn't exist. No Monday, no Tuesday, no Wednesday, No Thursday, no Friday, no Saturday, and no Sunday."

The customer was puzzled, not understanding what Hodja meant. But Hodja, being the clever and quick-thinking person he was, had a profound message behind his response.

Nasreddin Hodja's clever response to the customer's unique request conveys a deeper message about the impossibility of certain demands. Hodja humorously points out the absurdity of colouring the cloth with a non-existent colour and then suggests collecting it on a day that doesn't exist. This witty exchange serves as a playful reminder that some requests are inherently impractical or impossible. The tale encourages a light-hearted perspective on unrealistic expectations and prompts reflection on the boundaries of what can be achieved.

# Lies

During one of his teaching sessions at the madrassa [13], Nasreddin Hodja took the opportunity to impart a valuable lesson about lies to the children under his guidance. With a mischievous twinkle in his eye, he set out to demonstrate the deceptive nature of falsehoods.

Gathering the children's attention, Nasreddin announced, "Pay attention, children, I'm going to tell you a lie." He then directed their gaze towards the window and exclaimed, "Look, there's an apple!"

Intrigued, the children turned their heads to see the alleged apple, only to find an empty view. Nasreddin seized the moment to enlighten them, saying, "I told you I was going to tell you a lie. Now you can see how easy it is to trick people."

Nasreddin Hodja's demonstration to the children used a playful trick to illustrate the concept of a lie, showing how easily false claims can mislead one. By pretending there was an apple outside the window and then revealing none, Hodja highlighted the deceptive nature of lies, instilling a sense of caution and vigilance in the children. He intended to encourage the children to question and evaluate information rather than accept it at face value. The story underscores the value of discernment, honesty, and awareness in navigating truth and deception.

---

[13] A madrasa is an Arabic word that refers to any educational institution, religious or secular, and can be used for elementary education or higher learning.

In a small village, Hodja, a wise teacher, was known for his insightful answers to life's questions. One day, a curious villager approached him with a burning inquiry, "Teacher, what is the method of being a man?"

Hodja, with a mischievous twinkle in his eyes, responded swiftly, "My dear, what is not to know is of course the ear."

Perplexed by this cryptic answer, the villagers couldn't comprehend its meaning. Sensing their confusion, Hodja decided to shed light on his enigmatic words.

"Oh, what's not to know?" Hodja exclaimed, noticing their puzzled expressions. "When any man engages in conversation, he must listen with all his heart. But here's the secret: his own ear must also hear what comes out of his own mouth."

Nasreddin Hodja's cryptic response carries a valuable lesson about the importance of effective communication and self-awareness. Hodja's witty remark highlights the significance of both listening attentively to others and being mindful of one's own words. The tale encourages individuals to engage in meaningful conversations with genuine attention, emphasizing the reciprocal nature of communication. It serves as a reminder that being a true "man" or person involves not only hearing others but also being aware of one's own words and actions in the process.

# Old Grave

Nasreddin Hodja, always known for his unique perspective, shared an unusual request with his family. He said, "If I die, please bury me in the ancient grave." Perplexed, his family inquired, "Why do you wish to be buried in an ancient grave?"

Hodja, with a mischievous smile, explained his reasoning. He said, "If, after my passing, Munkar and Nakīr[14] come to question me about my life, I can confidently tell him that I died hundreds of years ago and have already answered all of his inquiries. That way, I won't be bothered with repetitive questioning."

His family was both bemused and astonished by his clever plan. They contemplated his words and realized the humorous nature of his request. Although they couldn't predict how the angel would react, they found amusement in Hodja's ingenious scheme.

However, one family member spoke up, saying, "Hodja, while your idea is creative, it is important to remember that honesty is valued above all else. When facing an angel's questions, it is best to answer truthfully and sincerely, for they possess divine wisdom and can discern the authenticity of our words."

Hodja nodded, acknowledging the wisdom in the family member's words. He realized that his plan, though amusing, lacked the integrity and honesty that should guide one's actions.

With a light-hearted chuckle, Hodja replied, "You are right, my dear family. Honesty is indeed the best policy, even

---

[14] Munkar and Nakīr, in Islāmic eschatology, two angels who test the faith of the dead in their tombs.

when facing celestial beings. I will embrace the questions with openness and sincerity, trusting that Munkar and Nakīr will understand the essence of my journey."

The family appreciated Hodja's willingness to reconsider his playful idea, recognizing the importance of honesty and integrity in leading a meaningful life. Nasreddin Hodja's initial plan, while entertaining, ultimately highlighted the value of truthfulness and authenticity. Hodja's understanding, guided by the family, that even in whimsical scenarios, maintaining honesty is crucial, enlightens us about the fable's moral lesson. The story reminds us to approach life with humour and creativity while staying true to ourselves and valuing truthfulness, guiding us in our worldly and spiritual journeys.